RAW.
THE
TRILL O'G

RAW.
THE
TRILL O'G

LADY K DAY

RAW. THE TRILL O'G
©2024, KAYLEE HANNAH
ISBN: 979-8-218-42812-9

First Edition, 2024

Printed in the United States of America

Edited by Anne Marie Wells
Cover Design by Michelle Mayhall
Layout Design by Janis M. Albuquerque & Emily Anne Evans

Self-Published with the support of CLI Books

DEDICATION
(HARD WORK, PLUS PATIENCE!)

For
Sydney, Billie, Ivory, Nala.
I am eternally grateful for your existence.
I love you more than words can ever explain.
You young queens are my heart in human 4m.
You are my
ever after.

Ever more,
Mama

This book is dedicated to my family, my tribe, the ancestors who left foot-prints behind, my flowers who've Sunderstood my pieces, the ones I've loved and lost, and those who've attempted to break me. I love you all.

For any who have dealt with the torment of their mind turning on them, the wounds of trauma, the living scars of abuse, loneliness, addiction, hopeless-ness, homelessness, self-doubt, or if you have ever asked yourself whether it is worth it to be a good person in this world, this book is for you.

Most importantly, to the MOST HIGH, the glory is Yours.
Finally, to all the versions of me, future, present & past . . . we did that.

With Love and Joy,
"Lady K Day"

TABLE OF CONTENTS

PART TWO **RAW**CUZZ

PART THREE HALLELU**RAW**

PREFACE

RAW. THE TRILL O'G

The title's meaning is open to your own interpretation. But, if this terminology is a completely foreign pool you're wading through, allow me to give you some traction to kick off with. I will first dive into the ending. I love when things are out of expected order. Unpredictable is life's way, afterall. That, and I am a big fan of Quentin Tarantino.

I digress.

The word, "trill" in the hip hop community, means the truest and the realest; the gritty, resilient, honest aspects of life. This term is said to have been created by those close to the prolific rap group, UGK out of Port Arthur, Texas. I was born in Texas and soon afterward moved to Los Angeles, California. My Texas connection is reflected in this word choice as it is where my story began. If we want to get a bit deeper, a trill in music theory is a quick up and down switch up between notes. You can see the metaphor there, I am sure, as the song of life has its own unexpected, rapid ups and downs.

One of the toughest parts of my life was when I was a teenager entering young adulthood and much of the darker poetry in this book was written during this period. I was staying in Louisiana, right outside of New Orleans. It was just after fleeing an abusive situation and living a chaotic, homeless existence for about half a year. I went to stay with family down South to see if I could get my head straight. But it didn't last long as I am Cali all day, and I missed the beat of the streets I loved so much. Although not enough time to say I officially moved to Louisiana, it was enough time for my cousin, Serg, who was originally from Texas (also staying in Louisiana at the time) to infuse UGK's influence into my blossoming list of hip hop legends that I have carried along with me throughout my life. For this I will always treasure our time together and have a special place in my heart for 'Nawlins.

If you cannot tell by now, I love hip hop. This is one of the reasons I am called, "K Day", after the L.A. based classic hip hop radio station. It has been said that hip hop is the reason I am still alive, and still single. Nothing and no one (besides God and my babies) have ever caused me to fall as deeply in love as this genre and culture has.

"But, uhh, back to the lecture at hand. Perfection is perfected, so I'ma let 'em understand" (Dr. Dre. *"Nuthin' but a "G" Thang"*, 1992).

Next we have the phrase "O.G.". For the folks who are unfamiliar, "O.G." is an acronym for "original gangster", said to have been coined and first used by certain Crip sets in Los Angeles. About this I will say that some of the best humans I have ever encountered; those who protected and guided me in positive ways when the ones who were supposed to, were unable to or failed to do so, have been affiliated. But don't get it twisted, I have deep respect from and for many hoods. It truly is all love. But to leave these Black and Brown Kings and Queens out of my art would be sin and including this phrase in my spin on "trilogy" is in remembrance of their impact on me.

The way I am using "O'G" is actually different from the "O.G." acronym, but it does sound the same. My meaning is, "of the G". Yes, I am a woman who is a queen, a mother, a lady, and an artist. But I am also a "G". I realized I wanted to be a G when I was 17 years old and I am proud to say 17 years later, I know without a doubt, I became one.

The "G" seed was planted in my brain by the first man I ever loved (RIP Noe aka Nips). He blessed me with this idea of who I would someday aspire to be on May 20th, 2005. We were at Noe's cousin's birthday party (Watts up, Mari!) in Lynwood, CA. What a night! We danced for hours on end, laughed 'til our bellies hurt and smiled like never before. I doubt I have ever had as much fun as I did that night. It was one of those gorgeous spring "a blink before summer hits" Cali evenings that feel like freedom is yours to hold onto forever.

I sat on this sweet Scorpio's lap and I asked him silly, curious questions, (probably
because I had heard the song, *"Daddy, I'm in Love with a Gangster"* by Knightowl earlier that day).

> *"Babe, are you a gangster?"*
> *He replied, "No, I don't bang,"*
> *"Are you a thug?," I asked.*
> *Again, "No," he responded.*

The exchange was reminiscent of the DJ Quik song, *"You'z a Ganxta"* who coincidentally is from the same hometown as Nips was—Compton.

I continued and asked, "How would you describe yourself?".
He sat back and thought for a few seconds.

  "I'm a G," he said.

My eyes widened and I thought what a perfect word to choose. I encouraged him to elaborate. He explained, "I had that environment around me to easily get
involved in the gang life. I chose not to. I could have been and done a lot of things differently. I'm not perfect, but I always had a mind of my own.
I noticed how those around me got into things I never wanted to experience. I've been around the life and I know what's up. I know how to move and I know I want something different than what I grew up seeing. I have love for where I am from. I have love for my people. I have respect for that way of life. But I am no thug. I am a G."

Right then I fell even more in love with him.

On that starry night so long ago, a blur of corridos, cold brews, loud cackles, gritos and bass heavy rap cuts blasting, my first love unknowingly set the outline for what attributes I would grow to value in a person forever:

Standing firm on the foundation of being proud of where they are from, reflecting on their past experiences in a healthy way while not being so chained to that identity that they don't dare branch out. Although their origins may not be fairy tale stemmed, they are realistic about their roots, and aim to live outside the cages of stereotypes and statistics so they can fully bloom despite any rain that may come their way. I love people who are supremely confident in who they are at their core and who they have become as a result of that history, not despite it; those who see and love themselves clearly throughout the entire process. This is what he embodied for me.

The last and most important piece of the puzzle is OG also stands for "of God". I live for L-O-V-E and if that ain't the TRILL OF GOD, then what is? I hope that message is conveyed inside this creation I have poured *mi corazon* into.

Therefore, I stand today proud to declare, I am "K Day" and I am a G.

During the process of writing this book, I added "Lady" to my stage name as an ode to my mother who is known as the "Lady of Light" and to "Lady Day", Billie Holiday. I named one of my daughters after her and I have received comparisons to her when I perform which is the ultimate compliment to me. I discovered her music at age 15, which was when I started writing the poems found in this book so I find her presence in my journey necessary to honor.

With that said, this book of poetry showcases the trill of who I have been, who I am at present because of all the moments stacked up leading until now, and the hope rising like the Sun inside of me for who I will become. This is me, RAW.

Inside this book live vulnerable poems, therapeutic songs, heart filled raps, real stories, and raw thoughts to narrate the wonderful, exhaustive, roller coaster ride it's been to get here. I hope something within these pages inspires you in the ways I have been inspired by the incredible souls I have crossed paths with and all the plays life has thrown my way that I've either fumbled or caught and ran with into triumph.

Thank you for reading, imagining, and holding on with me. I pray you enjoy the inner workings of my mind, heart, and spirit.

Genuinely,

Kaylee "Lady K Day" Hannah

RAW

LAST ST**RAW** PRAYER

Friday night
Rare, silent car ride

(Deep breath)
Prayer
God, I don't know how much longer I can go without letting go.
This wounded heart somehow is about to leap with no 'chute.
After *50-11* lifetimes . . . I know it's too late and too soon.
Picking up where we left off;
I can't understand how impossible can feel so right.
Souls in step, hearts in stride, cards aligned.
This unexplainable bond, I remember it like yesterday.
How has it not died?
That has to mean something, right??

Prayer
God,
I know this just started, again.
But I have no choice. A voice inside that is not mine
is urging me to utter aloud this

Prayer
If it is Your will that we continue . . .
(Deep breath)
then I ask this

Prayer
Wherever he is tonight, whoever he is with,
(Deep breath)
whatever he is doing,
I won't ask. I'll never know, but You know.
If this is meant to be, Lord, place an undeniable sign
directly in front of his face tonight—
something that will make him think of me,
only me, just for a moment.

(Deep breath)

Prayer
Maybe it will be a CD case he passes;
Art on a wall he catches a glimpse of,
A song, a phrase someone randomly says.
Only You know how You work.
I'll never find out what this sign is, but I know You're listening.
You feel my pure intentions.
Make something cross his path tonight, Lord, which will
carry no question.
This is my simple, solemn

Prayer
I ask for a reminder of me. I pray for just one instant.
That's all I ask, Lord. If this is not destined, please let us
let this go quietly, gently.
It's still early enough where we can get by without much damage.
I have a

Prayer
If this is not it, please don't let either of us walk away with heartache.
We'll accept it peacefully and depart in one piece,
finally in opposite directions once (again) and for all.
Thank you, I love You and I trust You.
Amen.

Continues driving in silence
Sighs in release
It's in Your Hands now

—Arrives at destination—
Walks in the door
Headed to be seated
Hostess makes a last second, unexpected change in direction
Whatever detour comes my way, my heart is at peace.
Gratitude

(Deep Breath)

Looks to the left
It's . . . *him!*
(Deep Breath)
I am seated directly in front of his face
in a city neither of us live close to,
in a restaurant neither of us ever go to.
Inside this moment, my prayer is...
WOW.

I'm in—ALL in.
Soft landing, crash,
I'm all in.
I'm Yours,
for life.

(Deep inhale)

(Exhale)

Prayer
Here goes
nothing.

[VCR Fast-Forward]

—5 years later—

Prayer
Thank you, Lord,
for now I look deeper into the Sun without wavering.
Nothing left to lose has strengthened me.

(Deep Breath)

Prayer
Father!
He threw away our jeweled, treasured Kingdom of forever
for the distraction of shiny fool's gold.
The devil's mine is his to keep.
Questioning

Prayer
Lord! Why?! How?!
My mate lost his soul!
Chose to forsake his checkmate
in a fruitless search for greener lawns and feebler pawns;
opened so many doors,
welcomed in every demon, danced in the fire &
laughed in my face as I wept.
He never knew the tears storming from my eyes
were less for my own pain
and more from grieving the loss of respect
mourning his death. The "him" I set on a pedestal—
The ledge from which he leapt.
He thought selfish desires
would lead to everything he ever wanted.
Joke's on him, as the enemy cackles. Game, set, match.
What he chased equates to all he already had.
This pit in my stomach takes root as I dread
the day he feels it too.
Despair
(Deep breath)
Last straw
Prayer
Send me a sign
one that I cannot ignore.
Let me know You'll heal this galaxy of emptiness he left me with.
Lord, I let it all go to let it all go.

Please let me know following Your lead was not in vain.
Time to release a future I will never claim;
toss back into still waters a past we can never get back."
Trusting

Prayer
Wherever I end up tonight,
Whatever I do,
Place a sign in my face
which draws me away from everywhere I've been,
anyone I've been.
I feel destroyed but because of You,
somehow I'm still here.
Driving blindfolded in the dead of night.
How can impossible feel so right?
Please guide me in the best direction.
Final release

Prayer
Lord,
Here goes
EVERYTHING.

Friday night
Rare, silent car ride

(Deep breath)

Prayer

CRAWL BEFORE

I have a tendency to get way in over my head.
It's one of my biggest flaws.
I go all in!
Never thinking twice,
thoughtlessly blowing bubbles
through the eyeball of a needle,
which is all fine and well

until . . .

I account for the size of my lips.

QUEEN OF HEARTS

I've got many hearts.
Each one sizzles a little differently.

LOVE DRUNK

Wandering past an abandoned antique shop,
I recognized this spot from a series of dreams nearly forgotten.
Flashbacks of this place randomly haunted my days.

So when I encountered it on a lonely walk to nowhere,
I knew unquestionably I had to go inside.
The eerie site's tattered sign taunted me.
Its Mona Lisa's smile invited me.
I was meant to be here.
Instinct imploring me to turn around, a hissing curiosity led me on.

I peered through barbed electric wire,
stepped over rocky clusters, rusted hubcaps and shattered glass.
I may have noticed fresh, glossy tears strewn along the pathway,
heard running footsteps fleeing in opposite directions
and possibly multiple women sobbing . . .
but I pretended they were raindrops and the romantic sound of the wind.

I headed onward, scaled the tall, brick wall
and bypassed the sleeping watchdog.
For such a guarded place, I found nothing odd in the fact
that the door was left wide open.
It should've been my first clue.

They all told me to stay away from this side of town,
but the allure of its song on that cloudy day called to me
as if my own personal siren had manufactured a melody tailor fitted for my ego.
I couldn't be pulled away by 1,000 Clydesdales.

I entered fearlessly, perused the aisles.
The dusty lamp shades with moth-eaten fringe had personality.
I used the sleeve of an heirloom garment my family
had generously gifted me,
as a dust rag
to clear a spot on a large mirror with angels carved into its frame.

(My reflection was always disappointing.
Eighteen years and still I was not used to who greeted me when I took a look
expecting to see myself.)

Then, suddenly, a glimmer caught my eye.
The loudest, silent beckoning I'd ever heard.
My riled up, childish reckoning rustling up reasoning to go against
the grainy grit of my gut,
gritando forewarnings plummeting onto earplugged drums pulsating
to their own groove.

You stood out among the miles of others that looked merely interchangeable.
I knew something was different, sensed we were destined to journey together.
You may have seemed like an ordinary ceramic cup,
but something said you'd been through more than most.

I felt your history, longed for your wisdom, couldn't wait to drink in your story.
I perceived glory in your mosaic of brokenness,
loved how the chip on your shoulder reflected the Sun.
I yearned to sloppily gulp in all of you nonstop.
Nothing could quench my thirst.
I took you out of that place. You were far too special not to see the day.
I made you a home behind the door I never let anyone enter before;
this place, my safe escape.
I set you on a shelf in my most intimate and vulnerable room
where the light entered through a rose-tinted, stained glass window.
I carried you around my neighborhood proudly,
held you tenderly and brought you along on my travels.

I stared at you, in love with the reflection I saw.
Your cracks enhanced my flaws.
i was hooked.
i filled you with my best.
i ignored that the only sustenance i'd received since we met
was the bleeding of my lips as i embraced your severed shell.

I couldn't figure out how the more I poured into you,
you remained continually empty yet somehow grew larger each time
and required more of me.

Endless taker, I was once overflowing until
I became obsessed with giving you as much as I could get my hands on.
When I saw even a drop of increase, I fell into a frenzy convinced this was it.
It burdened me not. I had so much to share! What was mine was yours!
I couldn't see you were depleting me ceaselessly.

You replaced my conscience, my confidence, my sense of direction,
until the moment I finally filled you all the way up.
I knew this would be a day of uncontaminated joy, the day of "enough."
I decorated the house, applied the blindfold, dimmed the lights and waited
for the "Surprise!" as you grabbed what you needed and snuck out the door.
I refused to open my eyes to see you had taken all I was made up of.

The buzz was intoxicating in its deafening disappointment.
I was love drunk on the tasteless void
we exchanged
for my soul.

THE **RAW**DACITY

The curtain has been drawn
to reveal a certain truth
They said the truth hurts
but I didn't have a clue
that finding out said truth
would leave me feeling so used
Burned betrayed and bruised
but it's nothing I can't handle
Every challenge holds no candle

to volcanoes I be paddlin' through
All my life I've been abused
from my value being sold, an
innocence stolen
Never realized I was golden
From day one
told that I was nothing
So if I want the world all to myself
then to myself I'll stay until

I make my fantasies finally
become too real to steal
and I find an honest man
Don't look at me as if I want too much
just do the best you can
to understand that all I've had
is lies lies lies
broken promises
slaughtered dreams
and more than I deserve of life.

SURRENDER

The light that
    used to shine
        has faded.
The sparkle in
    the tell-all eyes
        has died.
I'll remain
    silent 'til
        my last breath.
My voice of
    strength, now a
        mere sound jaded.

    Remember me fondly.
    At least 'til
        I am dead.

DELUSIONAL

I lived for love
      and love was given to me.
I died for love
      when love was ripped right from me.
I fought for love,
        I lied for love,
I thought that love
        was worth to try for love.
Lord, was I mistaken.
        Now I find that I am breakin'.
My perception has been shoved into reality.
        Did so much not knowin' what I was doing.
Chasing after love
      when love is just illusion.

BRAVEHEARTS

Blessed are the purest hearts
Fortune favors the brave
Evil arrives to keep sin alive
And rip yo' soul apart
Try as they might
Diggin' at chosen ones
Only puts demons in graves - R.I.P.
Warriors, keep eyes to sky
Word to every Star Eye See

All's fair in love and warfare
Hers and Him set
Battle Tims prepped
We 20 toes down, that mean 4 pair

Ride 'til the wheels fall off
Off the rails, like nosebleed seats
Those mean we
Top level, will not settle

Tied (Tide) 'til the seals pop off
Hear them wails (whales)?
Air fuels fire, fire sparks water
Feel hot kettle

That's Tea 4 daughters
Sword for sons, 2 sharper than 1
Angel number 421,
"What's done is done, battle been won.
Devil can't conquer
Armies of angels,
Holy Spirit, Father and Son

PRINCESS FREEONA

I am magic
Divine and unsigned
Y'all can't have this
You see how that shine?
I put in elbow grease to get this aligned
Princess slaying dragons and heroines stay away from static

Aye, it's passion over here! Fun and ecstatic
Give you one taste and you'll keep comin' at it
Like that black habit (heroin)
& Yeah, I see the effort. It's not that I can't match it
Just too far ahead now and I can't move backwards
Real shit - Stuff that into your Backwoods

See im at this peak in my life, take a peek in my life:

Don't care to speak my mind
I ain't got no beef with time
Just making peace with mine

Dolo keeping busy, no one moving with me
No need for co-signs, only heat for cold signs

Creamy pie, sprinkles right
Curling, dotting, c's and i's
Clearing spots in all seeing eyes
Vanish into fog, leave ya (mist) mystified
Real eyes realize I couldn't
Miss if I tried

WILD RIDE THROUGH A SLEEPLESS NIGHT

Do not travel backwards on Achilles' heels.
Marching band taught me we must backtrack at times,
but to *Stay Alive,* Bee a Gee
keep eyes dead ahead
& stand firm on tippy toes.
Full body momentum, suspension dependent on our smallest appendage.

We brave the roughest terrain led blindly by timing alone
& sustain blasted notes of bloodstained fury
with the contained, unfazed breath control of a mute monk in a monastery.

Let the bars burst open as measures unfold,
dead men's tales untold
spring to life or fall victim to the night
when you find they brought only
unseasoned judgment
& slander to a knife fight.

All in the chain smoking name of maintaining mundane, distant glimpses
of the sunrise's surprising surmised storefront,
slanging morphine dunked hope
at the forefront of your mind's eye.

Don't mind I.
Hopeful & hopeless I've been both.
I've trekked invisible ice storms in a ripped coat.

My ancestral tongue drags the track's curves; bends the corner.

A win's an honor,
but an L always taught me more about the scars that adorn her.
Digging deep within, I zoom by
catching up to a turtle's bluff
I piano jazz and spazz on elephant tusks, leanin' into every turn,
gulp my murderous,
luxurious,
excursion dust from the purple cup.

Would've succeeded - exceeded life's grasp
if it hadn't been
for those meddling kids!
I'm backpedaling while still snatching wigs.

Yes, in fact,
I'm an unstable handful
of overly faithful mixed nuts;
a prideful spinning vinyl made up of crisp cuts!
An unkempt, un-kept, too-friendly medley.
I'm hell in a bread basket, no butter.
Opposition taken under on tombstone flight.
Catch it quicker than a snapshot mem'ry of when wombs owned rights.
Witness the spillage of my village of brilliance.

Grab yo chance while you can,
before that stone cold ice cream cone has time to melt in ya cast iron pan.
The clock strikes 12. Carriage to pumpkin leads to finding marriage ain't nothin'
if it's to the wrong person.

ALL ringed hands on deck.

All ringed hands on deck!
Revealing that hand we hold so close to the chest
will cause jaws, balls, and curtains to drop
& yellow brick roads lead to nervous, turbulent Wizards of Oz.
While you left clicking grass ain't greener,
cracked glass heels,
disclosin' you have no space to call a place like home
alone and the specs are just homegrown specks of Orion's belt
liquidated then regurgitated 'til reverberations are felt.

These are simply the truth-filled cards I've dealt.
Sipping submerged ice rocks
drowning in Jack as I pock
-et Jacks
and ball then bounce, no study sesh, yet I ace the test. My brain's a mess.

Outlawed, yet *Still I Rise* to
beam with pride. My verses provide worthy rides.
Dreaming up Machiavellian, Rockafellian, peanut butter and jelly encrusted
lava cake splatter
of my imagination's
creations.

BASIC GIRL LAMENT

I am bound in these bones,
trapped in mounds of flesh,
prisoner of mortality.

A ball and chain drag from my ankle
to "protect" me from danger –
at least that's the angle.

Routine and this mundane existence
suffocate me.
My spirit misses the open air.

I envy the golden eagle who soars in revelry
while this desert eagle glides alongside me.

Long legs long to run free with the cheetah's majesty.

Pine to smell the pines and take anything to the extreme.
Turn this whisper into a full blown scream.

These confines never suited me.

CONGRATULATIONS,*

When you play someone with a good heart & pure spirit,

twist up what they've done with good intentions

into something only you would think to do,

have them constantly apologizing for sins that would

never even cross their minds, just to pacify and keep you,

Chile,

just know, you've only played yourself

out a lifetime of blessings

& sunshine.

*On one of the East Coast's most famous hip hop radio stations, there is a segment called "Congratulations, You Played Yourself" where the radio personalities talk about stories in which people do dumb things and end up putting themselves in horrible positions. This title is a nod to that segment on Hot 97.

UNFORGETTABLE GHETTO TEMPLE

There are those lonely souls who still drive down a familiar,
abandoned street
when the nostalgia hits.
They'll tell whoever's nearby to listen,
"I ever win the lottery, I'm buying that one back.
Only place that ever felt like home.
I soaked up all its joy 'til one day it was gone.
Ate greedily off all the sweet fruit trees until one day
they were bare.
I never tended to the soil then blamed the weeds for being too loyal.
Too busy chasing cheap thrills with no use for roots.
I didn't know how precious them homegrown treasures were
Until I left . . . Man, I've been cold ever since."

A K DAY USO-KU

(6)
(8)
(5)
SYLLABLES

People be like flowers
They smile in your face & they cry
When you look away

POETRY STYLE CREATED BY:
THE USOLOSOPHER, MOLIMAU ANDREW FATU

DWINDLING

I have become
too accustomed
to inconveniencing
myself for the comfort
of others.
My fun sized body refuses to take up
most of my own
queen-sized bed
because it feels like an imposition!

Mind you, I sleep ALONE!

I have bent over backwards and
overly bent up my back
forcing myself into places and spaces
I don't belong in,
drowning in the middle passage between gravity and passiveness,
literally and laterally challenged. I
never fully rest,
never fully stretch. I'm
holding up the balance,
teeter-tottering
all night, flirting with falling
off the edge of the bed
so my imaginary, hypothetical,
"someday" partner will know
I'll go
above and beyond
to make sure
he feels more
than welcome.

Is this the type of man I'm subconsciously manifesting??
Someone who receives his comfort at the expense of mine without
blinking an eye?

Someone who wipes the bottom of his shoes
across my face as I lay flat like the mat I am, smiling docile
as I beckon him to cross the threshold of my ornately adorned door,
gutlessly, regretfully accepting
every speck of debris he tracks in on my freshly waxed floor??

Looking back, I can see clearly where this low self-esteem began.
I got so used to the idea of being the girl who didn't demand.
I grew convinced I would smother someone simply with my existing.
I trained myself to be ready and willing
to give someone all the space they could handle.
I knew how to efficiently become consumable,
imperceptible and sized for travel.

My disappearing act was sure to amaze.
All these tricks mastered to save face,
not mine, you see, but that of he who didn't think twice when
he'd humiliate
in front of a crowd then manipulate to make
me believe I didn't know how to behave when all I craved
was to bring peace into his guise of a successful pace.

Eventually, I perceived my thoughts to be worthless, chaotic pebbles
thrown jaggedly against the solid rock of his godly logic.
Redundant and awkward
is how I was seen by the one person I thought could see me.
I felt I owed at least to rush out of sight upon his command
and jump through blazing hoops
to ensure I don't kill the mood
because my presence was just that uncouth,
my essence that uncool.

I gave him what he said he wanted!
I became what he said he needed!
Even though each time I did,
I compromised my wants, my needs
in the influx of a ruckus fueled rush
to feed his ever-hungry ego.
No more effective than placebo.
Placeholder, origami crane folder,
never stakeholder on his heart
though I played my part,
I earned no points in his eyes,
not one molecule of love to show.
It's just not how these things go.

That's not how this game's designed.

As I diluted me
to purify him,
I saw the respect
dwindling
in his eyes
and mine.

PRIDE CRASH LANDS
FOR SIMBA

Don't let my silent pride fool you
My heartbreak roars loudest under the stars
Where you once made me purr into submission
& if you ever wonder,
No, I'm not over you.
I'm not angry.
Not sad,
Not confused, only disappointed.
In you? Nah.
You were just the beautiful vessel
Through which
I disappointed
Myself.

THE ART OF PULLING WEEDS

The art of pulling weeds
can be summed up in a few short words.
The most intimidating ones,
those you brace yourself for
come up out of the ground dangerously easily.
You fall backwards swiftly
because you depended on the weight of the
roots they do not possess
to hold you down.
It's the humble ones,
those you missed on the first few walk-throughs
that turn out to be
the toughest to remove.
Underneath the beautiful
are where all the insects make a home.
The most surprising find of all
is how a dreaded chore
ends up becoming
such a lovely reward.

SOLA

Be alone.
(BE)(alone).
No one knows
You're lonely.
No one will ever know
Unless you make it known.
But you don't, so . . .
BREATHE.

No one knows you're
Lying by yourself,
Lying to yourself,
Like,
You're not wishing
You could lie with one.

Chest, resting place for head, nestled.
Fingers gracefully interlaced,
Fresh faced,
Hair running amuck,
Wild coils unwrapped,
Soft and luxuriously free.
Exhale in curiously "me"
CHEMISTRY UNMATCHED.

On them so tough,
Legs locked so much - you stuck.
Hypnotic breathing,
So deep, the waist cannot stay snatched.
It's cool, tho.

These *"just the two of us"* moments,
Momentous,
We can make it 'til we cry,
We can make it 'til we fly.
Melodic tension builds, comfortably
Sprawled across butter bamboo sheets,
Eyes maintain contact,
'Til full lips meet.
Hearts in sync drumming beats
to Sade & WizKid on repeat.
Then in a blink, daydream
Makes its hasty retreat, recedes to the
Recesses that coin
These costly ways in which you think
Love is within reach.

No one knows the trouble you've seen,
No one knows your sorrow.
No one can see the daydreams you dream,
No one knows you're hollow.
No one feels the weight of
The yesterdays you never thought
Would see tomorrow.
No one sees you sink
Into unshared sheets
As you shrink so you won't appear weak.

Stop searching for the escape.
Instead, embrace "alone" fully.
Cuz, truthfully,
You're not fooling
Anyone.

AWARE

I play the fool
on the daily.
You love me,
I know it.
You need me,
just don't show it
Everyday
I play the fool

RUDE

The numbers on the clock
are getting blurry.
I've been staring too long.
The clock, she taunts me . . .
numbers changing
and still no phone ring.

HIGH QUALITY H2FLOW

The real gem is to let it all flow
The big lick is to let it all go
Finding peace in detaching from
what I had unease in
the holding on
Bruises left in shapes of fingerprints
on every inch
from every itch
I never should have scratched

My tracks outlast backs and
savagely ravage, damage and harm arms
Scarred parts of charred hearts
I so desperately fought to keep

Staying still,
I see empty dreams flee
as I deeply breathe
and recede the urge to disagree

I expected bitter sorrow to appear here
in this void I refuse to avoid

Yet instead...
I'm proud to see
I'm finally
FREE

MY TYPE

I was never one
to size a man up
by the size of him.
Someone pointed out
that I have a preference for
skinny niggas,
but it was never conscious.

At first glance,
I never first glanced
at his shoes, watch,
the print—nope.

I daydream about a man—
not with crisp J's & creased jeans,
but a worn out Bible.
I want that shit to be
RAN THROUGH.

I want to go through his pockets
as I sort our laundry
and find packets of Tapatio,
scraps of paper
covered in partially written poetry,
notes on how to enlighten the world,
and unfinished raps
scratched on the backs
of receipts.

WHAT YOU MIXED WITH?

What are you?

What you mixed with?

Nah, where you from? (my posture straightens)

You got Black in you? (you want some?)

I didn't know you spoke Spanish—You Latina?

Hannah? You half white?

You and yo' siblings look nothing alike!

But where's your family from though?

What are you?

It's NEVER
Who are you?

I am the dew drop that came
when my father rained
down on my moms with violence and hate

I am the bubble that burst when my mama prayed
for a pristine good girl with an easy to pronounce name

I am the feisty remnants that remain
from when my great-great-grandmother was chased
by rebels in Mexico then hopped on a train
and hid in a barrel to make it out alive
so we'd have a chance to be generations later

I am the burnt out jingle from the food truck on a
sunny summer Saturday on Rosecrans and Central

I am the sprinkle of hot sauce that spills on the asphalt
the one the hardworking elote man
does not have time to notice

I am the silent pride in not being tender-headed
I am the musical methodical mischievous opus
who my daddy ain't want
I am she who grew into everything he ever wanted to be

I am Ferngully the way I be talking to trees
I am the one got these men begging on they knees
But always and only after they leave
and see not everyone got heart like me
I am madre, mother, mom, mommy, mama, mamà, ma, mami,
mum, mummy...
Wwhaaaat?!!?!!
...Hi...

I am lying and saying I have plans already
but really I just wanna snuggle in my beddy
wit' some Sade playing, freshly shaved legs
washed sheets, candles aflame
and these 'Pac, "Rose That Grew From Concrete"
pages in my palms waiting to bloom

I am pogs
I am yellow power ranger
I am that 1950 Ford Mercury woody wagon
wit' the smoothie wheels
I am that surfboard sex waxed strapped up and ready to go

I am Lauryn Hill unplugged, Alicia Keys no makeup
I am the syncopation in a Rakim cut

I am sweet Arab rice and savory jerk chicken
I am using the leftovers to fill up some crispy tacos
with a splash of lime, con salsa de papaya y mango
y extra sour cream!

I am the girl that man said he'd waited a lifetime for
only to forget he ever said that
when he dipped out wit' some "yes" women
who could stay out all night with him
cuz they ain't have to get up Saturday morning
to cook for his children

I am the one who will achieve all my dreams just cuz you told me I can't

I am the one with too big, door knocker, solid gold, goals
which I spoon daily into an IV to keep me high

I am the massacred-hearted, hopeless romantic
I am the good luck grasshopper
I am the striped cat on her 9th life with her hand raised, smile blazing

I am the girl who picked up a shovel, laced up my Tims
and joined a construction crew just 'cause the notion was funny to you

I am the one who can see right through your facade
I am the one gracious enough to hold my tongue, smile and nod

To answer your question,
(because I always know what you mean)
My mind just likes to take a voyage
on a sea of questions I'd rather you ask

I am Blaxicanese (coined that myself)
Let me break it down
I relax my curled up identity in a collision of
"Proud Blxck Woman, but a Real Ninja first" syndrome, (I'm sick wit' it)
Persian / Lebanese by way of my beloved, saucy Granny
& Mexican Pocha, wannabe Paisa,
Con un random streak of Italian.
She pops up every now and then
to say, "I'ma do this life my way"
...güey.

Does that satisfy your need to label me?
Did I supply an interesting enough box?
Does my blackness qualify enough for these three week old box braids?
Does that quench your thirst to know precisely where the
texture of this new growth stemmed from?

Does it answer your curiosities about how I rollerblade glide so smoothly
like I'm light on my vernacular feet?
Cruise sweetly between workplace English to
Skate Express Chino slang to LA ebonics
to cool water Spanglish all in major chord arpeggios
without hitting any sour notes?

What am I mixed with??
You don't care anyway
The FUCK up out my face!

PASSION ON A PLATE

This pasta is passion on a plate
I play melodies with ingredients
Harmonize with homemade sauces
Bebop with herbs and spices
Scat with whipping cream and cheese

A pinch of pizazz
A dollop of sass

I improvise with sweet and salt
Crescendos of textures

A surprise at every corner, I jog and skip
Through colors and scents
Double Dutch oven bake and broil my way
Through ideas come to life

Jumping through conclusions, I bounce, rock and roller skate
with infusions

My palette stays on its tippy toes
My culinary experiments are daring, bold
I never play it safe. Go big or go hungry

Tight rope in combat boots and slides
Through fresh recipes and
Tried and true designs.

Pirouettes with pipettes and beakers
Disguised as sauce pans and blenders
A Kitchen scientist's tools

Paint masterpieces with spatulas, whisks,
and wooden spoons
Apron decorated with the splatters and
shattered ceilings of my imagination

I dredge and brew truth in my roux
The chase and excitement make me giddy,
 makes nostils flare and eyes roll back

What art will these hands create tonight?
Mouth salivates as I anticipate

That jazzical first bite.

BLUE DISGUISE

A clean record,
a false asset.
To judge one based on
documented wrongs
is the misbirth of justice.

No one is sinless.
So, a clean record
equals you haven't been caught.
Everyone should be a suspect,
especially those you'd think least likely to do wrong.

I suspect
those chosen to protect
are subject to project
an overwhelming sense
of authority

and
I object
to a badge and attire made in blue.

RAWTONOMY

Inside my heart
though I lie and say I don't,
I want to feel love again,
but I cheat myself
and settle for lust.

And when the dust settles,
that's when I'll be enough.
"Just enough" arrives late too much.
Cards face down, hearts up,
bleeding 'til I see fit.
You ain't never felt ocean like this, and
my waves ain't got no curl in they rip.

Ripped at the seams
I swore were forever war torn,
forlorn, so be gone.
You don't love me, it seems,
so move along

You've drained me enough
You'll never claim me enough
Bet what you waging ain't much
Done gambling my heart.
Just leave me alone.

LIKE WATER FOR CHOCOLATE
(I USED TO LOVE H.I.M.)

The third wheel grieves the loudest while stuck on mute
The wheels on this bus go 'round and 'round as if Gorilla Glued
To conveyor belt
Bound to this runaway train, my bated breath explains its
Refrain of pain to solitude's conductor
As if pleading to report its alibi.
I told you I was no ride-or-die.
Apparently, I lied.
Deceived my own resolve.
Convinced this false sense of independence
Came with an eternity's guarantee.
Now I realize its notarized contract was my safety belt
Erratically windsurfing just before impact
Collecting bruises, wounds and
Scrapes like stamps and Grandpa's cassette tapes,
I'm dragged from this rusted bumper.
Nostalgia numbers my days, a green heart's clumsy ways,
Foolish loyalty scoffs, my nerve's been lost
Seal can't be broke, when what I swore under oath, was
"'Til the wheels fall off".

MASK ENVY

Some days I stare in confusion
at people with smiles plastered on their faces,
laughter like thunder,
raining on my parade &
I ask myself:
How come I'm not like everyone else?
Or do they all just fake it,
and I can't tell?

ENOUGH

A cage is a thing of substance.
Let me spread the word.
Often times I'm punished
with pain I don't deserve.

Jesus says He's coming
but He doesn't have the nerve.
I had faith and still I'm suffering.
I've had enough of hell on Earth

SAVED

Just when I'm ready to pull
The trigger
An angel sits on my
Shoulder
Suddenly I'm free
I'm saved
So close to the end
Now my will is gone
Once I was deaf
To the words of an
Invisible God
Now I cling to His
Every whisper
He says He'll stay true to the innocent
Everyday he remains with her
Every day she lets go of
How wrong they all did her
Because of His grace
Every day
She finds herself
Less and less bitter

SO YOU'RE TELLIN' ME THERE'S A CHANCE!

Maybe—there's more to life than pain
Maybe—things won't always be the same
Maybe—this life will change
Maybe—one day I'll find freedom
Maybe—There is a God and
Maybe—someday I'll meet Him
Maybe—I am here for a reason
Maybe.

PART TWO

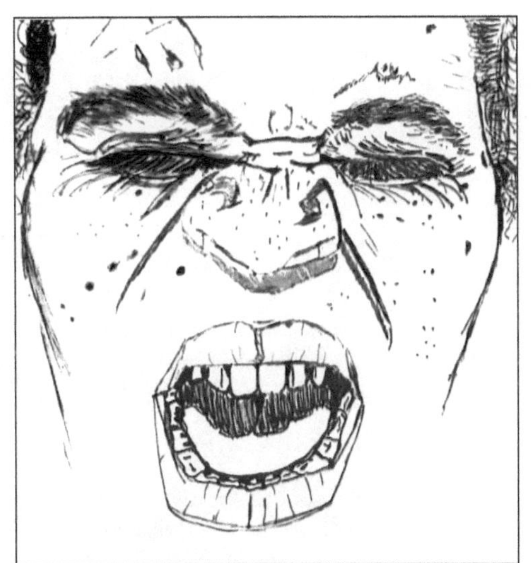

RAWcuzz

TIME WAITS FOR NONE

I've learned that time waits for none,
　And one can never go back.
I collect regrets by the stack,
　waiting to return to the past.
I waste life wasting chances
　for I'm much too immature,
Fearing the world's reactions
　'cuz I'm just that insecure.

Lacking courage, fearing change,
　hiding my soul, I waste away.
Because my life is empty,
　I think ill of those I envy.
I want to laugh, wish to live,
　long to tell it like it is.
I crave adventure and truth,
　then I choose the safe route and lose.

Someday I will find myself sitting,
　looking back on my life
with nothing to be proud of,
　no one to hate or to love,
Dissatisfied with my choices,
　eyes moisten, mem'ries poisoned,
I now see all of my mistakes
　only when it's much too late.

ONE DAY

PART 1

One day the lawyer told me this, though.
"The ways of the world gon' unfold ya, Sis."
"YO!! ??? !!"
I asked if there was reason for struggling.
This man said, "There's meaning in suffering."!
(Nooo!!)

I was guessin' he was faded cuz
them lessons fell out the matrix, Cuh!!!

Nevertheless, whatever he said
stayed in my head.
Probably keep me vexed 'til the
day that I'm dead.

Speaking of dead, this one day
I woke in sweat.
My eyes opened and I noticed Death.

I knew it was my moment when
he leaned over then
over the shoulder said,

"KAY!
Limits are being tested.
Faith is being measured.
Strength is being weighed,
You bettah get yo' shit together!"

Two weeks later, the corner of Western,
I was
slapped by reality,
trapped between catastrophes.
Shackled. (They can't handle me!)

Now I'm
face to face
wit' the day to day.
Sirens blast.
Silence don't last,
and a quarter of an inch,
is the length of a laugh.

(Lord, I ask:)
Why's it always for "someday" I'm livin'?
When I can't even see today, you feel me?
I know there's gotta be a way You buildin',
but I ain't even got one day left in me.

They thought they took my good from the beginnin'
They ain't know there's hidden sunrays within me.
I was killed but still
I live, I'm winning!
Gotta be at least one day left in me.

PART 2

I own nothing. I know nothing.
That's the best that I could do!
I do my dirt, hide myself from view,
and I slide them excuses, too!

I wish sunny dayz had lost me!
Tryna forget a time
when the smiles leaped off me.
Look what a good time cost me!

What's wrong wit' bein' wrong, I don't wanna be fixed!
I've adapted to insanity, so let me BE this!

Always got something to write about!
(Vague mem'ries of the nights I'm out)
and the tears bring dolla$, so what's the problem?!

Whole world got problems,
Stuck, corrupt AND fucked up tryna solve 'em.
Waste the days, fade away . . .
either that or find they way to the revolver!

But me?
Ima change the pace and break my chains.
Leave nothin' on the table, I might DIE today!

(Now, Lord, I'm sayin')
Why's it always for "someday" I'm livin'?
When I can't even see today, you feel me?
I know there's gotta way You buildin'
But I ain't even got one day left in me.

They thought they took my good from the beginnin'
They ain't know there's hidden sunrays within me
I was killed but still
I live, I'm winning!
Gotta be at least one day left in me.

BRIDGE

Now I'm pushin' to a place
past complacency,
but you might turn the page and see
the RAGE in me.
Founded my own street agency,
but freedom never come for free
and what can I change, really??

(Back in my one dayz . . .)

PART 3

I'd ask a few killas, and we'd plan revenge.
Taxin for my skrilla, we would mash that Benz,
but this game it's not as cold, man.
My Crips on the Ave. are growing old, and
so I lay low, and I stay schemin'.
I get high, so I'm daydreamin'
cuz I won't open my eyes.
I'd look to God but fear He closin' the skies.
So I put that low low in drive.
Time to GO for mines!
Re-up on coke for mines!

Life is not what it seems.
Why'd I let pain stay for free?!
He never paid me upgradin' fees!
But today,
I'm collecting rent.
I want him out, by the latest, 3.
I'm THROUGH with havin' nothing left.
If I ain't got nothing else,

(I've got this ONE DAY.)
Why's it always for "someday" I'm livin'?
When I can't even see today, you feel me?
I know there's gotta be a way You buildin',
but I ain't even got one day left in me.

They thought they took my good from the beginnin'.
They ain't know there's hidden sunrays within me.
I was killed, but still
I live. I'm winning!
Gotta be at least one day left in me.

OFF BALANCE SCALES

I can be at rock bottom, lowest of the low.
Still, I wake up grateful I didn't wake up...
as you.
I've gone so far on this path that
even if I wanted to turn back,
I can't.
Best to keep moving forward.
Your disrespect, those evil winds
have blown away the footprints I left in the sand.
I dropped breadcrumbs but they're gone now.
You picked them up to toss to me when I
was starving to death and I thanked you,
kissed yo feet, massaged yo head, fed you freshly picked grapes
while you feasted off everything I was killing myself for.
You bought your status with my sorrow.
Wimpy gladly drained me today with a promise of payment tomorrow.

It's the toxicity for me.
It's the audacity for me.
It's the hand-to-hand exchange of pain.
Same time, nigga, same time.
Underhanded motives.
Stand up for ya man.
Stand by ya man.
Ride for ya man
while that "man" never stand on
the ground he swore up and down he was ten toes down
solid on.

Yeah, it's the
overstanding for you, but never understanding for me.

And now you say it was good while it lasted and you wish me well???
Man, I poured my whole life savings down your wishing well!!!!

. . .
Oh well.

RAWCUZZ

DIVIDED STATES OF RAGE

They stay teachin' us
Don't bite the hand that's feedin' you
True meanin' was:
Don't fight the hand that's beating you!

Final pursuit to cock, aim & shoot,
That demanding OUR rights . . . Equal to
Wanting THEY CAKE
& to eat it, too!!

They say wit a straight face and a razor sharp edge –
Here's a coward's lube –
now stroke their ego Blue
& give their racist heart head...

Want you to stare in their eyes,
Cuz seeing you compromise
That pain you can't deny
is what makes it meaningful.

We just tryna to stay alive,
Being agreeable.
Not tryna end ya life??
Mind them Ps & cues

See, there is NO safe place
Cuz they screaming date rape
After they just finished fucking you!
& you WONDER why I'm cynical??

Their fearful life, the steering wheel they hide behind.
Crash course, driving blind.
Hate us cuz we see the truth
As we die inside . . . thinking WE the fools.

SENZA SPERANZA ᴇ PARANOICO*

How can one person alone
make a difference
when everyone else is against them?
Never knowing who to trust,
if ever there was a trustworthy being.
Power kills morals.
Financial security kills guilt.
Everyone's looking out for themselves,
and those who aren't are alone.
All alone!

Working for what's right,
against all odds. Stupidity? Or valor?
Never succeeding cuz the world
always brings them down.

Anyone could be against you,
so . . . suspect
EVERY
ONE.
It consumes you.
If you still have some
bravery left to go on,
they wipe you out
before you even take your next step.
making it look accidental
and the world is none the wiser.

Everything's a scheme.
They're always watching.

* *"hopeless and paranoid" in Italian*

DODGED THE RAM

To the One who's got every One figured out
Rerouted the main frame, held the frames of countless mirrors
Up to countless faces of crowds of shameless names
You've beat the code. No One can get One up on the One who's
Moved the chess pieces across all the boards before any One
Has had a chance to set hands on them. 10x out of 9 you're
Proven right. You've heard all the songs unsung. Ain't nothing new
For you under the Sun. Beautiful, Beautiful.
Now you can rest in the piece of your cave, knowing no One can
Desert or disappoint you. You had no faith in them anyway.
We all live down to your expectations.
Your hope rests, jet sets and resets in
One solo, sole, Soul alone. You can control the movements and
The narrative on your own stage, no need for connection.
You can play all the characters without correction.
Thank goodness you didn't come out to play.
Thank goodness you didn't show your face.
Every One's gonna do what they're gonna do despite what they say.
Game, set, match - Cracked plans hatched. I should check before
I wreck, but fate eventually drips from my mess.

Salud to you and this message, along with my best:

Not everything has a deeper meaning needing the oracle's reading.
Some beings just need feeling.
An outpour of energy toward
Outthinking, but can you outsmart the heart?
A matrix of a mind, yeah, that's nice.
I sincerely loved the One you hide.
You came into this world alone.
But to my heart's conquer and divide,
I had to accept with a sigh,
You'll never risk
Leaving it otherwise.

bRAWL

A stream of consciousness
A beam of confidence
You hit me in the chest
With eyes wide open
Still, mouth stays shut
Keep my enemies near
Empty threats don't make me fear
Lord goes before to stop opps
Before they ever prep for war
Drained yet I stay ready for more
Laid back, but I can bust back
And you'll never notice
Seeing clear out the Hocus Pocus
Kill 'em with kindness, disrobe him with jokin'
Laser beam thinking, Red beam meaning.
Playing nice while I choose my moment
Let you think I'm clueless, so it's wide open
Drop by the OG spot, counsel with the Kings
Why was I trippin'?
Really ain't no thing. Energy shifted
Come home you can tell I'm different
But you won't admit it. Guard's up so I let you hit it,
Just as I predicted, you fall back, I'm on the attack.
Nah my mind wasn't in it but I cum on command
Wasn't me who abandoned our love, come on man!
Can't turn a hoe into a husby, nor a Queen to a bum B.
What you thought this was, g?
Runnin' barefoot out this bitch - on to lusher lands
Betrayal forced my hand
Our aura was golden, ahora it's broken.
Had to take a stand. Trust me -
Becoming the Big Homie
To my own man - never was the plan.
How you think you winning if you lose me? You chose
you. Now I choose me. What's done is done, T.
Sue me.

WITH**RAW**AL

I would rather feel the orgasm
Of ripped insides
And the sting of a stitch
Than to flawlessly play my hand
Sacrifice my humanness
And take flying leaps without a hitch

You said, "don't hold back", you "want it all"
"Not just the light and the laughs"
But I hesitated and I waited
Because I knew to fall was a trap

Finally I ran to tell you I was done playing games
I thought you'd take it as an invitation and not another round
Lowered my pearly gates only to unknowingly seal my own fate
Okay, I became everything I said I wouldn't
But did you not do the same?

Laid out that blue carpet just to pull it from under?
I was Lightning to your Thunder, gave fullness to your Woneder
I shake my aching head at the foolness - foolish, foul, folly
To believe two lone stars could join in union so galactigodly

But I thank you for showing me you do exist
I never asked to keep you, only to find you
Now I can move on knowing I did

Thank you for reminding me I still am me under this mask
I still have this heart I thought I lost so long ago
To love like I never have, to cry like the levies been broken back
Inside, I have more than all of that
To rip the seams and take a stab, muddy, bloody, etcetera
If you never heard me, know I've said it once. "I love you"
Now watch me erase our memory
As if it never was

PHMG

Please help me, God, I am NOT okay! But so help me, God, gotta find a way!
Please help me, God, I am NOT okay! So help me, God, Imma find my way.

Pressure's been weighing on me.
The weather's still raining on me.
But I keep it movin' through the rain and the sleet.
Can't let 'em catch a view of the pain on my cheek.

Man, y'all ain't really sweatin' nobody!
'Cuz when my electric rise, y'all could never take the heat.
Aye, my future waitin' on me.
Jekyll steady pacing cuz my Hyde'll cancel patience (patients)
if you can't pay the fee!

Levels keep upgrading for me.
Got Satan staying up late praying for me to slip.
I'm graspin' that clutch, he'll(hell) never loosen my grip.
Devil setting up traps. Bitchazz swearing I'll fall.
So it's balls to the wall now!!

Reasonless, unfaithful, even Jesus paid for Judas' sin.
Treasonous snakes, they'll kill you wit' a kiss - all for da paper.
(How meaningless fakes do.)
Shotgun seat, where the ruthless been.
Blow smokescreens of deceit, take truth for a spin.
Never foresee who could switch route and flip.
Jackknife kin backstab for crack pipe & ends.

For the record, be them ones you cruised in with who let yo' blues just spin.
While you crawled to the Nile for them,
you need a mile, won't even move an inch.
Stay intuitive.
Water your roots & live!

See, when I feel like an ant among elephants,
my animal element bubble up & when I lift my chin I
can button up my Pendleton.
So, when the enmity wit' enemies get imminent,
instead of missing out on president$, I step to
pickin' up my instruments to establish my precedence!
Remember,
the world would stumble without my excellence!

Lord, humble my embellishments so I don't miss my Genesis!
Please Help Me God!!
Please help me, God, I am NOT okay.
But, so help me, God, gotta find a way.
Please help me, God, I am NOT okay.
But, so help me God, Imma find a way.

Please help me, God I am NOT okay! But so help me, God, gotta find a way!
Please help me, God, I am NOT okay! So help me, God, let me shine today.

EXCUSES

Is what I created
just a mess?
Or do they call this
abstract?

Did I need to go
full hermit to rest?
Or was it just to
distract?

Am I to blame
for all the
fuckshit
I attract?

Am I paving
my own path?
Or just wandering
off track?

99 excuses,
but
the truth
ain't one

HIGH THOUGHTS

High
Thoughts
Pilots
Fly plots
Flies caught
Crime tops
Papas chopping
Block
Top crop
Crop top
Cake.

Apple pie sky
Mile high
Free sky
Frisky
Fried sky high
Hairy slick
Cheery slip
Airy slop
Cherry Pop

Cheers

FLAT TIRE

You are my pothole.
I'm tempted to drive right through you because
—low key—
the ride is fun and loud as hell.
It's a quick way to break up the monotony, but
—high key—
you'll fuck up my tires, and I need them shits
to keep me safe;
to keep me going.
Can't let you slow me down, no matter how much I enjoy the bump.
But you'll never change
and it's not my job to patch you up.
I'ma just buckle up.
Then stay my ass out these streets.

BREMMST**RAW**LUNG

Like thunder it rumbles
Under the empty page
Feet done made you stumble
Same ones that kept you caged
Like is it … rain puddles, or humble
That keeps you rooted down?
Shufflin thru yo struggles
Beat you into the ground
Solo huffin thru them troubles
It slowed ya movement down
Judgin yourself - gave ya
Inner voice diluted sounds

STEEL WILL

Why can't we will ourselves into love?
Why can't we force ourselves out of love?

I'm supposed to be in charge.
I'm supposed to be in control.
If my "I" is uppercase,
then I suppose
I should have final say so.

All of this should be according to my timing belt,
not your every move puppeteering my internal combustion—
not a conveyor belt of subconscious destructive actions that
my conscience has no hand in constructing.

If your every wish is my command, then why on
the other hand, don't my own emotions
(own implies OWNERSHIP rights, no???)
do as MY own wishes demand?!

    This is MY body!
    This is MY mind!
    This is MY life!
    This is MY being!

I belong to ME!
I call the shots!!
I'm KING KONG IN THIS BITCH!!!

So why is the direction I'd rather my heart face
not LAW?
Why is the surface of my Mythril-armored
heart so raw?

I fuse my flaming eyes shut, welded in love dust and stubborn rust—
        everytime I catch sight
of your sunlight—won't be having me out here,
blind and awe struck.

Yet and still . . . yo brilliance wills my eyelids
millions of tie dye kaleidoscope shades of no such luck.

Ah, fuck.

ON PARENTHOOD

Sometimes I hear you,
but I'm not listening.
Sometimes I'm looking right at you, but see everything else.

I live in my mind, in glitching, light speed traveling thoughts,
and it takes me a lot of fuel
to get back here to now with you.

I feel the energy shift when I've disappointed you.
Sometimes the guilt kicks me,
and sometimes I kick back.

There are times I force a second wind
to carry me into igniting understanding of
where you're coming from,
cuz you shine when you feel heard.

I wish I was the consistency you need
instead of the chaos that breeds.

Patience and focus should be Olympic sports.

SUN BLOCK

Sometimes, sometimes no matter how hard the sun's beating down,
I just can't feel the sunshine.
Can't feel the sunshine
Sometimes, sometimes no matter how much I know it's there,
I just can't see the sunlight.

I strain my eyes,
stare directly into the sky.
I stay out from day until night,
unload the dead weight from my mind.

Why must you hide from me?
Why do those less interested have no vision trouble,
no inner struggle?
Don't I deserve a glimpse?
Can I just get a hint?

Sometimes, sometimes no matter how hard the sun's beating down,
I just can't feel the sunshine.
Can't feel a thing, mmm.
Sometimes, sometimes no matter how much they tell me it's there,
I just can't see the sunlight.

PUSH

Push me
Push me down
You are the ignorant one
Actually think
Imma stay on the ground

Knock me
Knock me down
You are the unsuspecting one
Kicking me
While I smirk on the ground

Watch me
Watch me rise
You are the one avoiding my eyes
Because you know
I am the unbreakable one

TRAPPED

I'm trapped in a prison of ignorance,
but I never realized how thick the bars were.
How I long to break free.
How long I've waited to see a ray of light
so I might have some hope of escape.
I wake with misery surrounding my soul.
Can't see past this cage,
holding me in,
molding my sin,
controlling my friends.
Inside these brick walls, I try to walk,
forgetting about this chain and ball.
It rolls under my feet as I fall.
Not even a window to nourish my soul.
Solitary confinement cannot be good for me.
I weep and sob, but my cries do not reach God.
Still, something tells me to stay strong.
I pray something will drastically change.
There's only so much I can take.

CURSED WORDS

I was born in the year of the dragon,
fully immersed under the fire sign.
My mother's rainbow-blooded child.
Emerged from submersion
three days early; the divine timing aligned. I
couldn't wait to make my mark,
embark on my Maker's design.
From jump I was jumpy—rather, bouncy,
hyper and joyful,
honest to a fault.

I miss that girl, who grew up in shattered pieces
with the same fierce despair of Adam and Eve
missing the Earth-settling peace of Eden before the fall.
But life didn't halt. It couldn't wait to disparage my salt—
That calm, too soon showed signs of disappearing.
Tragic disaster lied just ahead.
The lies would take decades to come to a head.

My death arrived at the hands of one too close for comfort,
not by blood, but made so by even more deceit.
Wearing a mask, the truth was not so apparent.
He saw my body as nothing more
than the outlet for vile urges he had been preparing.

Destroyed for life, I suffered years of abuse;
a tornado of heinous torture.
I used my brain to escape into rain-filled orchards,
and the rules?:
Never tell a soul. Never cry.
I tried one time, in my toddler words . . .
It only got worse.
Words became my curse.
A dark secret of disgust—one I could never discuss.
One so painfully well kept, one my child's mind could never wrap
its baby heart around.

Words could not be found. Silence was my token sound.
I searched for myself all over the ground, broken, and unwound.
No words could save me, they'd all think I'm crazy.
No matter how hard I tried to fight,
screaming mind, silent eyes, deathly afraid at the same time
that someone would find the truth hidden behind the words I kept inside.

It's no surprise that words became my key as I was jailed
in this house of hell,
with no one to tell but my pen and pad.
Happy and quiet on the outside, &
within held lifetimes of sad.

Fast forward toward the first time I got black out drunk.
The lie finally took a punch.
The false house of cards
at last destroyed, erased like smoke.
When I came to, I had no memory of the words I'd spoke
but the heaviness in the air told me exactly what I'd said.
My childhood you read as normal and never containing dread,
was actually full of rape, torture, and a corpse walking through life dead.

You see, when it comes to words, especially those
you've waited centuries to speak,
an impulsive "Yes" instead of "No" will cause an addict to
relapse in a minute.
Words can take a turn and collapse worlds in an instant.
But words only do so much.
So although Karma would do its damage better than I could ever,
I clocked the bastard one—just for good measure.

LONG LINE TO HELL

Mindless
Zombies
Conforming sheep
Cattle
Follow the herd
So you may
Be lead
To where?
Where else?
The slaughterhouse.

GROWN FOLXXX BIZ

Grip my hips so yo hand
prints leave a trace

Then forget my name
Cuz you know I love
the chase.

Leave me be,

Then come back to put me
in my place.

MUTANT MORPHIN POWER STRANGER

After heartbreak,
nothing makes sense.
The cosmos laugh at my expense.
I play the fool.
The game of love's expensive.
The turmoil inside—extensive.
I've lost trust and found myself
defensive.
I snap at the drop of a hat,
been slapped by betrayal,
stabbed in the back.
My false strength finally cracked.
I am alone
wondering where I went wrong.
I get my suspicions on.
I get my detective on.
I get my defective on.
Insecurity,
immaturity,
I've begun to break.
Tried to keep the one
I love.
Instead I became someone
I hate.

CHEATING HAS CONSEQUENCES

I sat.
I sat and stared.
I sat and stared. Stoic wall.

I pat.
I pat the stairs.
I pat the stairs. Idle hands.

Down the hall . . .
Your shoes
Your shoes; bare pair.
Your shoes; bare pair, no blood at all.

I raised
I raised the gun.
I raised the gun and made that call.

It splat
It splat everywhere.
It splat everywhere ten feet tall.

FALLING IN LOVE WITH A ROCK STAR

Falling in love with a rockstar
is one part heavy metal ***Thriller***
to two parts: ***System of a Downer.***
Somebody Told Me it's a ***Killer.***
Bandana clad, cruisin in them FOB Chucks
Rhinestone coated with
reality checks
and ego bruisin'.
Think you lapping the rest,
whole time, you losin'.
Season to your own taste.

Hard to avoid being burned when
you can't wait to scrape the plate,
cravings got you staying up late
and impatience says,
you BET not let one crumb go to waste!

Clock simp-ly reads, "Time is running out,"
then it's ***Killswitch Engage*** to a ***HEART***
who don't wanna be saved.
It's a ***Wicked Game*** to play.

Two shakes of a lamb's tail & a ***Cheap Trick*** with ***snake eyes.***
Shake it up, shake it up, shake it up, shake 'em!
and ride 'til them rims fall off.
Yes, Lawd!

It's a seven-course feast of ***Nirvana,*** and that's on my mama.
A no-fail recipe, cooking up magical heights,
and that bass line becomes the rhythm to your life.

Stairway to Heaven ain't got shit on him!
Misguided WestSide explosions boom bap like *T.N.T.*
They say *"Ain't No Rest for the Wicked"*
& yo they called that one to the "t".
Top speed, nonstop, racing up every step 'til you regret forgetting
yo' eyes been set in yo' head
upside down.
This *Riel Wild Child* really gets yo upside—down
Going pound for pound only get heavier as them rounds add up.

Forget all sense of self, you just can't help falling in love—
especially wit' a rasta rockstar.
You'll dread locking eyes with the eyes
of this *Lone Wolf* once you realize
there's too many eyes/Is in the way to ever keep sight of You.
Falling in love wit a rockstar
will have you *Diesel* fueled by *Crimes of Passion. You better run. You better hide.*
The slightest compliment will echo in your mind,
Pent up penta gin & tonic scaling your memories' walls & Preservation Halls'.
Boysenberry *Pearl Jam* packed with action.
Poison every plan you had up until he happened.
Brace ya self for impact—*It's the End of the World as You Know It—*
and once you *Back in Black*
Ain't no going back.
There's no willpower to be found here.

Un-*Eazy*, Running on *E*, energy reserves starving,
thinking one drop of attention will have you overstuffed.
All Fired Up and inspired [stuck] with endless motivation
. . . for scratching at windows at 3 am
just to get a taste.

Dream On . . . Cuz you ain't never met a ***Dream Weaver,***
Sky high, firm believer
in bringin' the impossible to life.
This ***Crazy Little Thing Called Love*** be lethal—
Have you feeling ***Invincible,*** you'll leap off the nearest cliff
cuz you so convinced you can ***Fly Like an Eagle.***
But the aftertaste of that distortion is never far behind.

Falling in love wit a rockstar
will have you rocket power fiending, nose diving
this ***Crazy Train*** to ***Where The Streets Have No Name***
facing ***Guns 'n' Roses*** from ***Concrete*** and the like,
just for one like, one glance in your direction and
the ***Fat Boy Slim*** chance of connection.

Good times.
Go hard.
Welcome to the Jungle.
Party Like a Rockstar.
Nothing else matters.
Eat it, ***Beat it,*** and
Rock On.

Party on, Dudes.

. . . ***Another One Bites the Dust.***

SQUIGGLY LINES

You remind me of those squiggly lines floating across my eyes during idle
time. Hyper active ghosts who make me question my own mind.

Ever-present somewhere inside, they never truly leave.
They're always within reach. I decide to search for their existence
when I can no longer ignore their distance.

They move at a lazy pace coming right toward me, full of intention, pretending
they're here to stay. As I acknowledge their footsteps, they deny it all.

I return their half-ass efforts full force, (my ignited torch) and of course,
they flee. I should have just enjoyed their dance in secret.
I wish I had kept acting as if I hadn't noticed.

For as long as I can remember, I have longed to pause their movements,
only for a moment, so I could catch one true glimpse and call it mine.

I would soak in every glorious detail, keep every memorized
curve and bend sacred 'til the end; never to share, never for resale.

Some voice knows deep down they are uniquely mine.
No one treasures the tiny crumbs of attention they lend as I do.

They make mundane, lonely minutes extra ordinary.
They force me into the present.
Bring to my perception complex, yet, simple questions.

Following them back and forth may be imperceptible to others,
but I know precisely how much time I am spending trying
the exact same method, yielding the same, fruitless results,
never learning my lesson.

I know without second guessing they were made to ride along
for this fleeting, candle in the wind journey, yet it still hurts me.

& I kick myself each and every time for chasing something
built to run away.

ANTITHESIS OF NARCISSUS

It's an on-and-off, odd,
        predominant, predickament—
                the way I evade vulnerability.

I throw caution to the wind,
        but only in the direction
                of Rolling Stones who never catch my drift.

My egotistical, cynical,
        cyclonic, psychotic Twister
                breezes past all my Muddy Waters

as my repeated,
        past seasons show
                I should know better.

At light speed,
        I tear through the peaceful calm,
                leaving a trail of shimmering chaos in my wake

while knowingly
        avoiding the glare
                of my reflection.

TRACK 

It's become a running joke
that I hate to feel trapped.

I often wonder where it came from.

I'm not claustrophobic, though.
Well, maybe I am.

I don't put myself in small enough spaces
to find out for sure.

Avoid the risk, avoid the answer.
Kinda like when I halfheartedly
play with the idea of loving you...

just until you reciprocate,
then I pull the rug right from under you

a
n
d
f
l
e
e
f
u
l
l
s
p
e
e
d

in the opposite direction.

OUT OF MIND

Time to write again
On my own again
Off a full night of half ass rest
Gulp a barrel full of regret

I'm strong in my weakness
Loud in my meekness

The pen scratches the pad
As if it had a mind of its own

My mind is in other places
Idle yet wild abandoned child
I wonder where she's gone

WORN OUT

This world is cold.
Hard for me to swallow
Like choking on ice.

Pain after pain,
Hard for me to follow,
I'm closing my eyes.

Struggle every day,
Not knowing when it ends.
Find trouble in every way,
while losing all my friends.

To escape the battle,
one must mind travel.
Blow after blow,
there's not much more
I can handle.

THE PRICE OF SUCCESS

A false sense of security
paves the way for conspiracy.
I've been so unaware of these
"pure" friends with such impurities.
Now foes show similarities
to allies I chose carefully.
I'm stuck not knowing who to trust.
Deep-rooted friendships, now corrupt.
If I show a shred of weakness,
they'll seize, leaving me in pieces.
Crew's real tight when cash increases.
Through hard times, no one knows my name.

GRIEVING

Makes no sense. Does not compute.
I know every ridge and dip of your face.
Still learning your ever evolving spirit,
I haven't quit because I know it still exists.
I avoid pictures because the familiarity
of the face I know so well, the face I have
loved half my life, only gives me hope that
if I search enough, I will find you.
My mind doesn't comprehend
the possibility
that you cannot be found

RAWNCHY

Addictions
A brick ton
Can't just pick one

Pianos falling from the sky
No dodge attempts
Too concerned
They can still play
After crash landing

Ivory keys last
Intuition in tune
I divide up that half
For the quarter hand-to-hand
Math enthusiast
Lewd and crude be in
"Harmless" downfalls
Nudes and ludes relift
Seemingly "prude" demons

I locate the exit green
Circle back once more
Check if I left anything
Spinning them sand dunes
Singing them sad tunes
Unlocked some doors
I should've left alone

Black on Black I walk the line
Fool myself for a while
Too fun to flirt with cliffs
Vile desires
Engage me in
Rings of fire
Caged in sin
No excuses
Why I do this?

Spoiled with choices
Why I always pick the poison
Dream to break free
But peace never been me
Same old song
Why do these chains turn me on?

KILLSHOT

The sweat buds form
Another day on the grind
A teardrop flirts
With ideas of falling
I pay the fool no mind
A quick glance around
And a double shot of envy
Here's to the customers of
"Kick back"
I sold the luxury of comfort
In exchange for work work work
Back to the hustle once again
Times are colder than the figures
Inked in my skin
As usual here I go considering sin
It's become natural to resort to
Crime
Do what I gotta do to get mine
Otherwise
I face a lifetime of servitude
Or should I say life tomb?
To live for someone else
Is to die to myself

CHASER

All I know is
nothing.
That divine
feeling has escaped me.
The thrill was immense-
in the beginning.
Now it's
a fleeting memory.
I'm coming,
I'm running,
I'm chasing
after a dream that's already gone.
They say I can do
anything,
but I'm not so sure.
Desire is the root of suffering.
The more I want,
the more that runs away.

FOOFA**RAW***

I don't wanna be kept,
I wanna be FELT.

Energy too heavy
To be held
Under a belt.

I get in deep moods,
Dust my needs off,
Sweep my wants
Under the rug

Submerge then re-emerge,
Can't tell you why
I see a thread and then tug.

Can't leave well enough
Alone,
So I trap myself in spaces,
Easily escapable—
That's if I really wanted to.

Don myself in chains and tape
Then wanna complain.

I don't need to be kept,
I do that all by myself.

*foofaraw: (n.) 1. A great deal of fuss
or attention given to a minor matter.
2. Showy frills added unnecessarily

RAWDIOS.

I know
"I"
dissociate.
You tell me as if
it will be a shock.
I have always been all over
the place—most dayz
I don't recognize my own
face.
I lie awake at night,
ask God if this is my fate.
Tell me what I did to
deserve this pain.
I don't want to know what
the other me does
or just how many
 there are.

You think I'm worried about
the others you have?

Nah, I'm afraid of the others
I am.

You could never handle the
roller coaster
who is me.

She makes me sick, too,
but there's no eject button in this
driver's seat.

Run while you can,
I don't blame you.

UP CLUTCHING MY BLACC PEARLS

To the humans who broke into my garage:

Have you been watching our comings and goings?
Are you evil? Are you insane? Are you dangerous?

Do I . . . know you?

Are you coming back? Please don't come back—ever. I found out you broke
into my dad's garage that I take for granted and often feel guilty about. The
garage I told myself just days ago I'm going to spend more time in. But since
pops died, I can't bring myself to walk back there.

A psychic warned me a few weeks ago to make sure I lock up my car and garage
as someone may soon try to break in. He dropped some specifics about a
sudden increase I'd see in my finances after struggling for so long.

He was right on the money.

He also said I'm about to fall in love with my soulmate.

So by you breaking in, you've actually given me a glimmer of hope, along with
a shitload of fear and paranoia.

I don't think you took anything except for my peace of mind.
I would just like you to know, you did me a favor.

And if you come up in this house where my children sleep tonight,
I will graciously return it . . . with this motherfucking glock.

Can't sleep.

—*Kaylee.*

FOR LEOPARD

Empty bathroom floor with vomit on it,
tears run dry, wants to die, if she's honest
She's all alone, when he's gone, when he's home.
Coward knew a victim when he saw one.
Weak-minded, free spirit was the target.
She spoke Willow Tree like Pocahantas.
Cannot break away cuz then her thoughts spin.
Changed that number convinced she is off him.
Script is flipped—he shifts the blame right off him.
The lonely hits, she runs back too often.
"Even let you beat me, just don't leave me."
Begging—now he's got her where he wanted.
He plays nice, she thinks twice, then she calls him.
Cycle starts again—a happy hostage.

A FOOL'S REGRETS

These days, they're pages gray
This life, one rainy day
Too many stupid choices
For paper and foolish poisons

JAYE SHOMA KHALI*

I want to erase all the poetry I ever wrote about you.
But it's all I have left.

*"Your place is empty/ Wish you were here"
-Persian/Iranian phrase

CELIE SAID

Until you do right by me,
everything you even think about
gonna crumble.
Whoever said I was just made to be part
of your story any fuckin' way?

AMANGA*

First love, young love, always said, "Truuuue!"
Second love, twinflame, often said, "Truthfully"
Third love, soulmate, stay saying, "Truly!"

All them niggas Lies.

*"lies" in Zulu

VENOM

I oil my limbs
with the edges of your hopes and wishes.
My chosen dream is to distance you from sane decisions.
Buzzing with vile desires,
[Hennessy buzzed]
entranced with visions of your come faces,
humming laced hymns of your Sun praises,
I am your number one fan.

For your airy light fans the fire inside,
a flame I refuse to resist.
My every wall outnumbered, surrounded
by the storm I weather.
Wild passion knows no bounds when your
tender rain
blindfolds me and binds my hands.
Violent choke holds and sensual pain
become her
obsession.

Love, be my air, and if you can't,
make me explode as you take me under.
I could not care less if I drown.
I stand no chance.

You rose to drain nectar from the fruit I manifested.
Ambrosia in yo' kiss,
pain stained across my bliss,
and left upon my lips,
venom.

RAWMEN NOODLE

No rules.
No consequence.
Are those the ingredients
for raw passion?
No inhibitions.
No limits.
No fear.
Is this the definition
of ultimate freedom?

RAWORA BOREALIS

Rise and shine, Kaylee.

Where you think you is?

You've been 'sleep for a long time now.

Time to wake up.

Get up off yo' azz.

Get up on yo feet.

Time to do something.

Time to be someone.

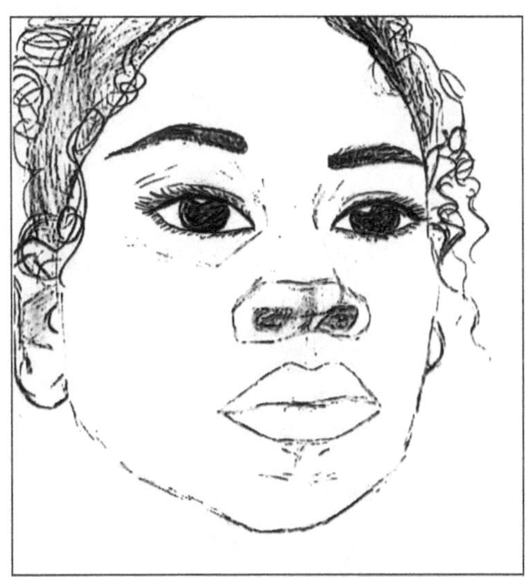

HALLELuRAW

COMING OF AGE, BLACK IN THE DAZE

Honey Child, 24-karat golden child, chosen child of God,
did it slip your mind as you sip yo' wine and whine ya hips this
shooting star lifetime does not grow on trees?

Sunshine, dip ya lips into this tea:
As you exist and breathe in,
do your Set and Rise Justice, SunKiss.
Don't stop Believin' that we arrived to birth on Earth sans compass.
Journeyed to this planet,
blasted on the surface imperfectly, perfectly purposed,
stacked, packed and strapped with a task to uplift, that's worth it—
just no road map to plan it.

The only guarantee, that unspoken momentum.
Moment to moment,
moving forward, pushing toward the end of life as we know it.

In youthful days, we'd see pendulums swing lazily.
Summer heat waves hazily babying our playful dreams.
Seasons ran long, sprinting calves strong,
from dusk 'til dawn, to infinity and beyond,
We'd tiptoe trot the furthest ledge hedged for the young.
Spinning our wheels we spun on edge 'til our whirlwind heads first
tried to dive, then belly flopped into window shops
displaying what we thought was "grown"
as that crisp Cali air filled our lungs.

Yet childhood travels would be far out done
by millions of mill of the run, humdrum, just-for-fun fantasies
leaping recklessly among Jacaranda leaves
roamin' freely through lavender and peonies.
As far as we imagined, ocean waves crashed with abandon.

The days dragged on 'til the dazed dragon breathed fire.
No pausing to think; sunscreen was for the weak.
We chased the heat and life's pace increased.
Passion's desire forced lead foot to pedal.
Lead to sharpen our focus,
peer pressure's hocus pocus was a plague of fear-based locusts
carving our hopes and blind vision one notch at a time.

Maturity's motive lent us drive to reach fallen destinations.
Barely alive, we became ghosts who haunt a nation.
No longer hidden behind childlike eyes;
insecure & broken, we'd seen too much.

It stung to find our buzzing hive was not enough.
Even with the honey sweet comfort it provides,
it refused to guide us through detours or
shoot ahead to shortcuts where triggers would reload.
Gullible innocence in a sense had to die
to teach those egos to decode stop signs in disguise.

We unmasked and de-robed evil
with fortunate happenstances & naked forest dances
single handedly dismantling circumstance's wiles
while wild, frantic people peered through spiritual peepholes.
They panicked but managed to steal and still take us for granted.

For the rest of our days, we'll stay incognito with this only goal:
repo all that we lost
to false amigos when our guard was down.
X's ran off with cheap shots, but we plot
value in flashes of beast mode.
It's all in how you handle...Struggling and Hungry. These lessons don't come free.
Unashamed, our dignity is not a game.
Choosing not to freeload off those who pounded these grounds before,
but forgot to share the cheat codes is how
divine composure's found.
This life ain't only black and white exposure now.
So, we must point and shoot every single free throw
before the final buzzer sounds.

HUSTLE and RENOVATE

Rebuilding an inner house
takes vision, diligence, guts,
gumption, pain, & patience.
It requires fire.
One must possess a true blue tested conviction in
the reality of miracles,
countless rough drafts of
cerulean-tinted blueprints
& a muddy, bloody pair of steel toe boots.

The work is a worthy investment.
It is not simply fighting
to uncover great bones.
It's resurrecting a world wonder.
Future generations will marvel at
its evolutions,
& birth innovative societies
based on its legacy.

Children's children's children will stand mystified,
dazed at how it's still standing.
Archaeologists will study its many
destructions throughout the ages
& draw inspiration from its reconstructive phases.

BLACKAZZ SHEEP

A story's protagonist is in fact a
lamb in wolf's clothing.
Forever ignored unforeseen impact abhorred,
She was born sensing the foreboding.

Nocturnal creature in flight,
not a soul heeds her foresight.
Still, as her trust erodes she won't implode.
She hones her gift in tact and with that,
she sees all that hides at night.

Immortal non-combative,
hidden, corpse reenactments
make you assume for yo' satisfaction
she'll retreat and retract when
observations and statements are made.
Who you think you 'bout to play?

You Extra!
Extra! Read all about it
I'm a quiet ninja floating.
I is she. She is I, and above all the bullshit
we fly high intertwined.
Did yo twisted logic (k)not realize??
Silent killers do the most damage in a fight
&
I'm not as dead as you would like.

Nah, I just dimmed my light for survival.
Schooled by the hardknock life that raised a scapegoat child,
Mother Betrayal birthed my will to rise up but lie low.
Y'all not finna lie on my life then pull me under ya tidal wave of shame.
I REFUSE to sell my name for a title!
Before I drown,
I'll burn this entire bitch down in rebellious fire!
& That's on my mama.

For doing what's right I've been left so low.
Now I trek this path solo.
Barefoot and scarred, but head held high though.

Y'all etched these lines in the dirt.
Y'all dressed me in this villain's skirt.
My voice of protest is mistaken for a troublemaker's disguise.
Don't be fooled.
We just happened to wear the same size.
Not much choice—y'all couldn't handle me nude.

I howl all I've seen into the moon
where none but the stars listen—they just glisten and mind their business.
They not ones to interject and rush to correct.
That's why I sacrifice rest to spit my war tales to outcast bats who never
question the truth or second guess who's who.

Did y'all know the road to hellfire is cemented with good intent?
That's why I don't just speak about it- I BE about it.
See, the ones I needed most were never there when I had to bleed about it.
But I'm still here, and cowards don't know what to make of that.

I'll don this coat of the many shades of black
you choose to use as false proof without regret
cuz just underneath
resides the lion-hearted discarded hero you never met - me -
plus a bullet proof vest

Me? Lose sleep over what you think? Honey, please!
I ain't gotta prove a GOT dayum thing
and yo' judgment is something I never sweat.

See, I'm like a bad azz ballerina—them ones in the fluffed up dress?
While I'm making my moves and I'm spinning the block,
I keep my neck on swivel and my eyes on lock
on my dreams, integrity, and nothing less.

Cuz I know
one day you'll discover
the REAL devil
be the muh fucka you'd never expect.

Soulfully Yours,
KDay Muhfunkin' Hannah

FOR J. WARLOCK

I have this friend — tall drink of water,
lost in thought.
Stomach rumbling but will not
admit that he's hungry.
He be struggling wit'
wrapping his uncooked vegan bacon heart
around a too spicy, jalapeno pepper world
housing a creamy, yet tangy center of
an almond-based truth.
He's raw — just how I like 'em — dressed in distinct,
but unseasoned.
Not one reason to lie,
out of reasons to hide.
Everything he's tried just won't stick.
Sittin' in a cast iron
skillet waiting for the heat
to rise, but can't seem to find
the will to feel for a match.
Still reaching out, but closing his eyes
wondering if that's really the way you
meet your match. Or must you
meet yourself first?
He makes me wanna open up my
prized cabinet,
the one that's been gathering dust;
Pour some of that leftover allover...
That good shit that angels huff.
Remind him how flavorful life can get
if every time you peer over your shoulder
you'd stop focusing on how high the chips are
stacking up and falling over.
Yes, this life can be dark and disastrous,
but you'll never get to feel the fireworks
sizzling and crackling

from inside the package.

ABRAZOS DE CACHEMIRA*

She brings in warmth I've never known,
one that feels like cashmere.
Blanket that envelopes all of me,
as a blessing fully covers a persistent striver.

She climbs up on my lap and throws
her delicate arms around my neck.
The radiance of her love brings
to my attention:
I have been freezing
this entire time, but never noticed.

No, that's a lie.
I remember when my
teeth were chattering and lips were blue.
I fiended for even the slightest passing
of sunlight through nimbus nests,
but it never came.

Over time, my reality hardened.
I forced myself to forget
what warmth truly felt like

until her
& her + her
& her.

*"Cashmere Hugs" in Spanish

TRULY

I wonder if you know
I pray for you
I wonder if you care

If I found out you didn't
I wouldn't stop
I believe in the power of
prayer

YO, YO.

No shame
No holding back
Ima be who Ima be
Iron packed lima bean
Mushy, gushy and solid
Chew on that
All of me
Not her
Not he
Not they
Simply
Complicatedly
Topsy tipsy turvy curvy wishy washy taped up mess like heck
like WOW
All of my
Fullness
Emptiness
Sweet 'n' sour badass AND chicken shit
Facets of a whole azz Black pearl enveloped ruby encasing diamond
A cracked one anyway
But it's still values at a GRIP
A GANG OF FER' y mas
Pentagons in a flying soccer ball
Black and white
Both extremes of the spectrum
Suspended in the wind
Expelled through midair kicked and kissed y abrazada, chiquiada, traviesa!!
My heart is who She is
Ima let her be
Ima set her FREE
Jesus said whoever wants to be first must be last
He washed the feet of His disciples which was unheard of
To be the highest you must be not only comfortable with but love to be the lowest
Let go completely of pride and ego in exchange for a new outlook
Humility and love go hand in hand with power and strength
Think not?

Waste not want not . . . and what not
Don't waste a trace of ya love I surely won't
I'm good to those who love me AND to those who do not
I tend to love you even when you do not expect it and
ESPECIALLY when you do not deserve it
But I do I go with the Sanskrit of my feelings
I FEEL fully pop that lower pooch button
Cornbread stuffed
Down to my core like magma
Magnetize reenergize empathize yeah that's alright with me!
A man I once loved told me that was called GodBody and I embraced it
Drawn to pour into those whom my soul tells me to
I am neither desperate nor thirsty

Nah I pour into you because my cup is overflowing
I love fully Baybee!
I love fool-ly
Both eyes opened wide with no reciprocity in mind

I will never regret loving or being good to those who I can see do not love themselves
Maybe I am in love with poison but it is only because I am fearless
I know with every cell inside of me I am stronger than your bite
My quest now is to love myself this strongly as well and wherever I question
God is my answer
His treasure dwells within my well

Yes loving me sometimes includes creating something from nothing or resting
Sometimes as simple as indulging in . . . hope
Choosing me over you for a season
But my love will never evaporate
For which match's flame can dissolve the ocean?

If you've never heard this before please hear me
When I tell you
I LOVE YOU
I love you

Te amo
I love you

No strings
No doubt
No way
You or I or yo momma or yo next door neighbor's goat
Could destroy that love
It is yours
Fully

Digest that

ECLIPSE FREESTYLE

My higher side is
on the rise tonight!
Go inside to coincide,
plus and minus
energizer vibes (ayeee!)
Creator lead the way,
my survival guide.
Ooh she a fire sign?
Yeah, she taking flight!
Adjust twisted thoughts,
been concealin' my flame.
I bust every shot,
I'm not unleashin' blanks.
Can't afford for even one hit to miss.
Hit record—you gon' wanna get this.
It's a
season of change,
there's no reason to wait.
OUT—been released from my cage.
DROUGHT—but still feeling the waves.
HOW—you think I'm speaking to greats
without increasing my pace??
NOW—In a hurry to put worry in its place.
VOWS—married to divorcing insecurity
SituATE legacy up on my plate.
SHOUTout the name, you gon' remember the face.
Visionary.

ROOTS

If you roamed the globe you could say you knew me.
Distant yet mysteriously familiar,
I am next door's sweet creamed corny essence
wafting through kitchen curtains.

Inhabiting a TRILLion spacials simultaneously,
my specialty be
dwelling en demasiada galaxies miscellaneously.
Alien even at home, a pizza planet unto myself,
I set up shop. Exit dew dripping tents barefoot,
suedehead journal in hand, crinkle wrist beads stacked and jingling,
& seamlessly enter buzzing communities.

I feel right at home conversing with the natives.
Although we don't speak the same language,
idiomas en idiosyncrasies sync easily.
I adore converting to local tongues in ungentrified circles of worship.
I become a taste bud for unexplored flavor,
an addict of unrestrained behavior.

Future siblings welcome me con brazos abiertos.
Washing hands of judgment,
first impression "D'Wayne the Rock" eyebrows expunged.
No room for concealing truth. We trade airbrushed airs
in exchange for open minded, beauty-ful, blended melding
of free reign, uncensored love.

No matter what box I check,
or in what labels I've in the past settled,
every union I enter will always be racially, inter-

twine slipknotted into the unbreakable thread
of who I am. It tugs at the delicate balance of
who appears in the mirror, whose spirit is with us
and who is inside my head.

I once thought I belonged no where
until I realized I belong everywhere.
I am ME swiftly slipping between portals
despite the bipolar porosity of my hair.

It's a gift to be allowed access into varying places.
This must be why I quickly understand any language.
I learned early the importance of listening intently before I leap to speak.
Feverishly gathering missing puzzle pieces
to see if they fit within my blank spaces.
I collect phrases,
habits and overlooked quirks.
I am a Mod Podged collage of everyone I have ever crossed paths with.

The remnants of my history are scattered about the Earth
in iridescendant blood deserted among deserts.

My polycultural story is fragranced by
the comfort of the food I cook.
I cannot stick to one cuisine!
I grapeseed, coconut oil fusion, grease my way into the room,
nonsticking to only one nation under God,
My origins are divisible though not always visible.

I bleed Red Black and Green, fully alive, streaming in blue hope.
Cruise into classic car shows,
'Cente belting perfectly timed with the LA Times,
I "Volver y Volver" right into Impact Zones like the Benny I am,
belly up through waves of belly dancing anklets and hijabs,
protecting what precious beauty lies underneath.

Throwing back "Tragos Amargos" in my '91 Bulls throwback.
Rice and beans (Red, Black, refried and fava)
Hummus and Pita,
Tupac and Biggie
Juices and berries
Sophia Loren, Maria Felix and Dorothy Dandridge.

I am a woman of many worlds.

I revitalize yo' spirit and nourish yo' soul,
transport you everywhere but never steer you wrong.
I eradicate you from the chains of your comfort zone.
I am Tres Leches, Tres Flores, (Dahlia, Calla Lily & Leopard Orchid)
Dipped in the Sacred Trinity of Tea Tree, Shea & yellow stick melted down
Cocoa Butter as
Father, Son, and Holy Ghost light my way.

Lady of a thousand flavors...
if you hunger for what I wish to place upon your plate,
you may salivate on this . . .

I taste like Neapolitan.

FLYING HIGH

I don't question when I see feathers floating by that no one else seems to see
I trust my dreams
I don't question when my angel number shows up LOUDLY
when I am secretly doubting everything
I smile in the face of each flower I pass
No one questions the tanager's song nor do we
correlate the frequency with how high she can fly
Singing calms my spirit and I belt it for inner security
I blast RRR because real recognize real
I savor every flavor of favor upon my life
I bird's-eye view it all from a guardian angel's angle!

RECLAIM

I'm coming for everything I lost,

everything I desire,

everything I wildly dream of,

and then some.

It's all mine.

That certainty is certainly
cuz every blessing I receive
ain't just mine.

I've wasted enough life waiting in line . . .
It's my time

1 OF 1

Artists have graced her ceilings with elegance.
Legends have walked her grounds.
She is the foundation of
      curve shaking,
         earth shattering,
            cage rattling
movements misinterpreted as faults.

Angel-scented, meditative holy waters rain down in her garden.
                  These cookie cutter luxury models
                    ain't got shit on Eden.

APPLE SCENTED CANDLES AND HOT TEA

Journal Entry

Here I am
the aftershock of a girl who NEVER had the patience for a cup of tea,
    a bowl of soup, etc.
PATIENCE . . . PSSSH . . . LUXURY, more like.

Widowed and single mother, minimal daily help, village where?

Let's be real. When did I have the time or how about the ENERGY
to put on a pot of tea.
To sit and actually be able to enjoy these things while they were still hot,
not be interrupted and savor a quiet moment?
I convinced myself I never even liked these things
because, at the time, I thought
I couldn't have them.

Now that I actually can, now that I make a way, I appreciate them more.

The babies are no longer babies.
The emotions and stuff fly around here at times.
Yes, sometimes it is loud and frustrating, but not hopeless.

Not as lonely as it once was; the more we blossom, the more I lean into their
friendship and insight.
In many ways it is a new type of enjoyable and on many days, peaceful
and safe in ways I
have never known.

These children empathize, understand, communicate at a new level and
lately, so can I.
You can say we grew up together. I re-raised myself as I raised them,
learned to nurture the child inside as I learned to nurture them.

We live in more space, in some ways less work, in some ways more.
It's a job not to clutter up and the upkeep is overwhelming at times.
Sometimes less physical work but more emotional and mental.

But all in all, we are falling into step with the stride of our life after being
in discord for so long while the world went carouseling around us at a
completely different speed.
The judgmental opinions about why we couldn't keep up aren't as loud anymore.

Now is now, and instead of comparing what was or what could be,
        I am just excited to be free to embrace this one moment

starting with this cup of tea.

TRUST

I am right on time
Give thanks to the Divine
Everything I dream
is already mine

LETTING GO

God help me use these wings
in all new things,
and for the ones that have
grown old,
make me bold enough
to wave them goodbye

TRUTHFUL SPOONFUL

All the could'ves, would'ves, should'ves
are what ISN'T.
Put your energy into what is

WATER THROUGH HANDS

Now that I've found you,
please don't go away
without me

& if you must, just
please don't forget
about me.

RAWTHOR

The toughest part is to start the verse
To struggle first is just part the curse
Trust the process and spit bars in spurts
The hunt for words is the darkest search
'Til you stumble where the artist lurks

UNSTOPPABLE

You can't stop a person who's overwhelmingly Grateful—
Dead in the eyeball of a tornado.
All you can do is delay their journey for a sec,
even throw a tomato or two.

You'll think you've eliminated their pathway
but all they'll do is adjust to the rhythm,
& embrace the Slow Jam to draw
more intricate footprints in the sand.

Then when you rejoice in rain falling down
on the masterpieces they created out of pain
you'll look up and wonder why the hue is fiery black.
Only to find it is raging volcanic ash - an eruption
disrupting your destruction of their song,
still echoing from dungeons.

At this point, all you can do
is watch helplessly as it seals
the prints they left behind
so they become fossils.

FOR THE REALEST

Hold me down
Without
Weighing me down
I can't wait
To see how high
We soar
That's why I'll never ask to
Be yours
God's clock is turning the tide
I ride skies
In no rush

For today
We crash waves
I enjoy being your escape
Maybe in the future
You'll call me your world
Cuz I was the one whose gust
Taught you trust
To lift yo feet off the ground
& As we intake the highest views
I'll be right there to point out where
Home is

Real recognize Real
Like souls recognize Soul
When I think of all a man
Should be
It's you
I first think of
We once craved to be
in love
Now we dream to
BE love

FORGOT TO BE YOUR LOVER

I'm used to standing firm
Walking, the narrow, solo line
Holding down the fort
Ten toes down to earth
Rock solid and unbreakable

The planet underneath at times
Gets shaky, trembles and roars
Reverts to Tectonic plates
Holding my stance, I
Steady my gaze and ride the waves

I carry so many with me, pack the heavy on
Balance is a challenge to maintain
But I sway into the groove 'til I like
The way my island moves

I like that it's just me inhabiting this lush
And sacred land. I travel naked and
If I fall, I have only me to blame.
But when it comes to you, I can't stand
admitting I'm afraid. To view you as a compass
is unexplored, uncharted plane.

I toss out accusatory, embedded questions.
The words escape before I can catch 'em.
To ask for reassurance feels redundant
And it makes me feel ashamed

You have just as much to deal with
Without me adding to the weight
I simply wish I could lift it
This feeling, even after all this kinship,
That you could at any instant,
Forget I ever existed

BASTET (EGYPTIAN CAT GODDESS)

This pussy is beauty.
Feline divine—the only one of her kind.
Ahead of her time, she sings from within.
Life giving, she rests in peace.

Owning her future, she lives in the moment,
She promises nothing.
You keep one night open
Not knowing she'll have you for life.

To die in the arms of a Soulful woman
is freeform falling into the abyss of fairy tale myths.
The thrill in her kiss, it's deeper than sin,
yet the weight (wait) is lighter than breath.

This pussy is beauty.

Graceful,
stretches of movement—
Baring toes in Leaves of Grass.
Explosive, BOOM!
Leaps of grace on a whim,
feasting on Grapes of Wrath
and rage
to escape
the rebel in you
guest performs on her stage.
She revels in drinking you in.

Unquenchable thirst,
quests and journeys to geysers unearthing the tension,
urging the further ascension.
Sharing in firsts, bearing your worst, indulging cherry topped seconds.

This pussy is beauty.

Blessed and reckless,
blazing seconds until we drown.
Dreamy, miles up under, an abundance of octaves,
together, asunder, thunder and stardust,
rounds on rounds of applause
clapping in steamy wonders of August.

Waking on faraway beaches, freshly painted parkway benches,
Sunray soaked, gently sprayed by the mist of her lips.
Lulled by hums of lullabies sang in the buzz of her throat.
Her sweetness drips, the balance tips—

Drawn by fragrant traces of mangoes and peaches,
Gravity dips, fingertips graze Zion in the midst of her bliss.
Gazing high onto doorbells of Heaven.
Baybee, fly on,
but tell no one
how high the peak is.

She's more than release,
She's the seed of belief,
She's the thief of peace,
Holding keys that unlock the deepest secrets of Sphinxes.

Suspended in air,
Carefree except
the slightest check for parachute straps,
Only to accept there's no going back.

You live in her now,
pulse has fused to her cadence.
The push of her pull is found in her radiance.
Patience puts her ocean in motion
and awkward is where she's the craziest.

She is not one to come on command.
Dive in now, but do not expect to land.

She steadies her crown.
She's ready and grown.
She's claiming her throne.

Her playground: wherever she chooses to roam.
In every world, her presence is felt and known.

If there's two things I know:
She tastes like freedom
and she feels like home.

SOLID

I am ready
to embrace living

To become Me

Truth seeker
Soothsayer
Strength teacher
Bricklayer

I feel solid as the Rock of Gibraltar

RAW AURA

These days require fire.
One cannot survive
on eloquence alone.
I travel far, and
I travel near,
and still I have no one.
Those closest to me
have hurt me the most.
All I can fight back with
are winter and tears.
I'm from a life
of broken promises
and lost opportunities.

Still

I will never
give up.

Ever.

COURAGEOUS DESPITE

Do you ever feel as if life is a
game in which everyone
knows the rules
except for you?

Sometimes it seems the only
option is to lay low and do nothing
because anything else seems impossible
even if it is the right thing to do.
It gets overwhelming.

But if it's between a sure comfort
and a near virtual impossibility,
choose the latter.
No matter how slight,
how improbable,
at least there's a chance for change.

WHAT WOMEN WANT

All I really want
is for you to look at me in awestruck wonder
Amazed at all I've become
You've been here since day one
Before I had a clue to who I was

All I really want
is for you to miss me when I'm gone
Say you love me at random times
just because you can't hold it in any longer

All I really want
is for you to be my best friend
and reassure me you're someone who cannot use me

To feel sorry for the things you once did to me

All I really want
is for you to stop looking for love
because you know you've found the one

To tell your friends with confidence I'm your one of one

All I want is for you to tell
the truth, *la verdad* (trust me, I can take it)
because it takes balls to be so raw
If I give you courage it means through it all, I'm worth it

All I really want
is for you to think of me as you get up and as you go to bed
not just when you want some head

All I really want
is something worth living for
The little thing I want is simple yet tough
I want True Blue Love.

TRUE BLUE LOVE

means...
the closer I get to you,
the closer I get to me,
the closer we get to God.

NO PUNCHES

Courage—get lonely than a muhfucka
While convenience posted on each corner
Compromise is ruthless
Thrives among the rootless
To survive just sacrifice ya honor
Yo conviction's no more than a bother
Mute ya conscience, that's shouting from within
You neck-deep, in stress,
Heat, wrecked dreams, debts weak-
-ened up the heaps you meant to KEEP buildin'

Nah. On some real, we can never let up
We can never give in
Temptation and exhaustion will keep knockin
But don't invite 'em in

Make confidence ya talisman
Charisma is the magic wand you fashioned
from the short end of the stick
Generosity's a triton
Fire up yo' sense of fightin'
Cuz it fuels yo' hot air balloon to keep you risin'
So keep on shinin'
with your torch of optimism
Self respect will be yo' shield
Keep ya head held UP&
Raise both fists high to guard from the lies & dysfunction
High beam your light
And baby, hold no punches

FORK.

I have been known to walk roads less traveled
and through my travels,
I've mastered unconventional.
My comfort zone is the unknown.
Always ready to go at a moment's notice,
I keep my shoes on.
Never get too comfortable.
There's always a bag packed in the trunk.
I hope you don't mind.
Stability can be so mundane;
security monotonous.
Promises feel so dry.
I thrive in unpredictable,
though I'll deny it to the bitter end.
The world is my oyster, and I always
fancied myself a mermaid.
I endlessly search for alternate routes
with no particular destination to be found.
When everyone is in,
I prefer to be out.

So, as I stare now
at two options before me—
two haunting staircases in the woods:
One, winding into a daunting fog, its mystery
thrilling and exciting . . .
I'm curious at what it means that I'm somehow
tempted by the one that scares me more.
The one I know from sky to floor
and every shortcut in between . . .
The familiar one.

RAWSOMESAUCE

I'm the type to put extra sauce on everything.
EVA
RAY
THANG.

Whatever I spit, create, engage in
BET it's finna be
ALL MINE.

My fingerprints are braggadociously all over whatever I've touched.
Signature thick lipstick marks are all over whomever I've loved like tattoos.

I explode and exude
RAW.   Alive.   High Larry Us.   Writhing,   Electric,   Calming,
Off-center,   Unnerving,   Swerving,   Reckless,   Ruthless,   Zen,
Darkest Chocolate Layered,   Blasting,   Blushing,   Still.
Dipped in iridescent destiny and dangerously neon.

If this is your tendency, freak-quency
Nature or hidden desire . . . Please

Make it precious.
Make it hideous.
Make it crisp.
Make it skip.
Make it brave.
Make it sing.
Make it scream.
Make it new.
Make it over.
Make it cream.
Make it count.

Just make it interesting.

Make it bleed YOU.
Make it ooze YOU.
Terrible,
Nasty,
Elegant,
Slutty,
Holy,
Tsunamic,
Gnarly,
Angelic,
& finger lickin' as FUCK.

Go there.
Then, go further.
Climb two poppy-adorned mountains barefoot.
Swim six gnashing, unloved seas naked.
Guitar strum your heart strings to the rhythm of your elevated pulse
After you've danced to reggae in the fire you created from your own ashes.
Rest in peace, bathe in peace, make love to peace.

Then go some more.

Or don't.

If that is what it means to

BE YOU.

SOME BEANS 'N' RICE FO' DAT AZZ

No matter the situation,
no matter who you engage with,
decide up front what you're willing to give out,
what your limits are,
and what a reasonable return for your output looks like.

The goods exchanged could be money, words, energy, connection, love,
favors, joy, time, attention, relief, pleasure, business,
understanding, compassion, empathy,
R-E-S-P-E-C-T.

Each and every interaction is a TRANSACTION.

Trust yourself.
Know your value unwaveringly.
Let no one talk you into unfair negotiations.
Take up space.
Train up your voice not to shake.

Carry yourself impeccably
&
Deal accordingly.

FRAWLIC

I have a dream,
Won't let go of me.

I chucked it off a bridge
To release
Its chokehold.
Only seemed

To latch more firmly
Into my seams (firme).

Unforgettable, untearable,
Guess that's unterrible.

No matter how many dives
Into depths without taking breaths,
Success won't set me free.

After all my kamikaze attempts,
Abandoned shipwrecks,
Scuffles, shuffles, rumbles muffled,
Spilled Holy Water mess.

1 of 1 + (negative anything),
Still = 2 Blessed

4 aces stay aligned in the deck.

Like child to mother's breast,

This dream holds me close to the chest.

HALLELU**RAW**

the bongos banging, claiming the room
tambourines a-jingling
organs all in tune
children singing in the choir
hands clapping, bass blasting
then suddenly...startingly
all
grows
silent
except for one sound
my
heart beat
volume increasing steadily
harder and harder it pounds
'til its rhythm consumes me
i'm lost in the vague
noisy
crashing
chaotic
stillness
in the frozen disorder
i find myself
unrecognizable
an unstoppable FORCE
an ever growing MASTERPIECE

and as the realization of self
becomes my environment
i stand
no longer shackled by fear
I welcome in the bongos
I greet the strings
Beckon to the beck and call
Of my song and dance
The praise of my love
Is on fire
Rushing mind has fallen mute
Contemplative
Grateful
From witnessing the scene
To becoming the seen
Transforming has
Transformed me
Serene
This sounds like
The epitome
Of triumph:

Hallelu
Hallelu
HalleluRAW

ACKNOWLEDGEMENTS
A B.I.G., JUICY THANK YOU
(SEE WHAT I DID THERE?)

To Community Literature Initiative and Sims Library of Poetry, Sims family, my instructors, T.A.s, and classmates, from the bottom of my heart, thank you! Your critique, encouragement and support affected the revolutionary evolution of this ugly duckling in ways beyond measure. When one of us soars, we all soar!

To Anne Marie Wells, my copy editor, thank you for your hard work and contribution to this project. Michelle Mayhall, my cover artist, thank you for bringing an idea in my head to life! To Janis Albuquerue, my book designer, I resonated with you from day one. Thank you for being so real and such a soldier! To Emily Anne Evans, CLI Book Manager, I cannot thank you enough for your advice, commitment and incredible attention to detail. I appreciate y'all very much!

To every person I met at each step along the way, I pray you know you are part of something grand and spectacular. Hosting events, sharing your talents, creating opportunities, and uplifting community is changing the world one mic at a time!

Y'all, I took notes! I toiled and I honed! I soaked in your every syllable! I studied your reactions, body language, habits, stage presence, EVA-RAY-THANG. So when I say you're a part of me, I really mean it because all that I observed can be found in beautiful fragments in everything I create.

To my Willietta, you believed in me without question. Please know how IMPACTFUL that was. To be believed, listened to and pushed without needing proof first. Before any of this made sense, you told me it was something I must do. Failure did not even enter your mind and that catapulted me into taking many leaps. I love you more than you will ever know. Thank you for always being an angel throughout my life.

JRieLA, I thank God for you. I'll always remember you as the first man in my life to keep his word without fail. When you told me you would do something, you always came through. You never made a promise you couldn't keep. Your art and work ethic are on levels of their own. You expanded my view of the world and taught me to never give up, ever. For that, you have my loyalty for life. WestSide!

To the woman who has shaken me up especially when I have doubted my abilities, and gifted me so many opportunities to grow, 'Drea, you came into my life at a pivotal time. I am so grateful for you. To Quannie, thank you for showing me how to grace and rock a stage with class, power and sunshine. You are a superstar.

Mr. Tommy Domino, thank you for being a kindred, bluesy soul who just gets me. Thank you for your support. Thank you for driving clear across the city to make sure you were in the audience for my very first feature and prioritizing my performances in your schedule. Please know I treasure our soulful connection and that your work means so much to me.

Speaking of my first poetry feature, to King Moe and Queen Brittney of Haus of Meta, thank you for giving me the opportunity to grace your stage at your Neo Soul Sober Social event! You helped me to believe in myself. Thank you for living a life which goes against the grain in the greatest of ways. Blessings upon blessings to your growing family!

Myron, I am blessed to have experienced your genius firsthand. Thank you for being one of the first to point out my writing was unique.

To AJ, thank you for teaching me to get up to my glamour.

Andrea, no matter how much time goes by, we always pick up right where we left off. You have elevated the way I carry myself. You are a rare and solid gem. Also, thank you for teaching me to fold a burrito, the countless laughs, and decades of friendship. Boots, Giggles, You and Karla referring to me as "Carrie Bradshaw" or "the writer" or you saying you think of me when you pass by a Barnes and Noble was on my mind as I wrote this book. I love you ladies!

To Valeria, God knew I needed me a you. You are rock solid, one of one. You make everything better than you found it. Your loyalty, your dedication and your hardworking ways are exactly what the Bible talks about when describing a Proverbs 31 woman. You are a TRUE FRIEND. Anyone who has you by their side is winning so I count myself blessed. Had it not been for the role you've played in my life in these past few years, this book would not exist and the woman you tell me I am who inspires you would not exist either.

Thank you and I love you.

Marta, you need your own book but a paragraph will have to suffice. I am in awe of your growth! You have dug within the deepest parts of you to acquire your essence. Your heart has always been pure gold. We are meant to support one another and hold a mirror up to each other's face when we most need it. My Sag Sis, I love you and I thank the Lord for you! I would not have been able to complete this project or break from certain ties if it weren't for you. You are worth more than diamonds and rubies. I love you.

To my Icy friend, "Diondre", you are one of the key men I know who seems to grow more confident seeing a woman do her thing. I am so inspired in being around your, how can I word this, "lack of insecurity" that my presence brings you. Your friendship and our connection is very special to me and I truly hope you know how much I respect our bond. Distance, time nor circumstance can break what we've built over these years. Thank you for always supporting and fueling my flame. You are a good man and a real friend. Love you!

To BAE, a spitfire writer friend of mine, I value your laugh, your journey and your words. Your mom is so proud of you. As a mother I can assure you she is. Thank you for being a person I can relate to and having such a beautiful heart. You deserve so many good things in life, and they're coming in soon. Get ready!

Carlos, you were the first guest speaker in my first poetry class. It was not an exaggeration when I told you I would not have continued this mission if I hadn't met you. The way you reacted to my writing and the way our styles reflected gave me the push I needed. Thank you so much for answering my random book idea texts at 2 am, guiding me, protecting me and making me jamaica. You are the rap poetry yin to my yang!
I got love for you! You have a special place in my heart for life. Whatever, whenever, I got you!!

To my peoples: Abby I love you with all my heart !! especially those who helped out with babysitting, carpooling, lightening the mama load, Addy, Ms. Toni, Steve and Jill, Laulie, Herlihy family, Susie, and many more for coming together as a village so I could pursue my dream when we realized this wasn't just a hobby, but a calling. Thank you so very much.

Stewart family, thank you for attending my Like Water poetry workshop. It was so cool that by chance we were featured in the video shot that day at the Cafe! You've always come through for my family. Your poems meant so much to me at that workshop, your presence at the Whittier Christmas performance, your life stories, projector movie nights and inviting us to visiting your neck of the woods inspired me to write outside of the box. Love y'all.

Brandon Lee, you know what it is. A lifetime of us can't begin to fit but I'll say this. Wouldn't have made it this far without you. You're my protector and my guardian angel. I thank God for everything we've been through. You're one of the few who really know me down to my darkest sides and still go hard for me. That is God's love rooted in a friendship. I'll never stop believing in you, so you can't ever stop. If not for you, then for me; if not for me, then for the memory of Cline's sexy legs LOL. "Jk. But seriously." Love you.

Granny, you are my bold inspiration and teacher of Womanhood. You live life YOUR way. You introduced me to God, taught me to pray and were the first to show me about writing down the family history. You continually share our story with me in our conversations because it's a part of you. You are one of my very best friends and you do not realize how much I value your input, your encouragement, and your love. I admire you so. You are a RARE woman, a visionary, and my saucy Granny. Thank you for being brave enough to choose our Porkchop and to share with me y'all FIERY, PASSIONATE and FUN love saga. I miss Grandpa everyday but our memories keep him here with us. You both were the MAIN CHARACTERS in your lives and your adventures inspire me to always remain the LEADING LADY in my life.

MomMom and Papa, you two, Lord. I am inspired all the time by your LOVE. You have shown me firsthand what true love looks like. We have shared the best laughs, been through some tough times, and you somehow are still two selfless people who always find
a way to encourage, support and love on others. Thank you for being a beacon of light together and being there to show me it's okay to give more than is necessary, especially when you find your counterpart. Two kindhearted, loving people can find each other in this world and create more happiness and joy every single day because they are unafraid to love fully. That is what you have taught me, so you are my hope.

Uncle Chick, thank you for being in my life. You have made strides in ways I don't think you realize I notice. I admire you so. I enjoy being in yours and your

Queen's presence. Your home provides this inexplainable, calm; a peace I have prayed for and am feeling more and more with each day. Thank you for being that person I can depend on. Thank you for being the man that you are and living out God's love. Thank you for being the definition of family. I love you.

Babyfather, thank you for the role you played. I'll always root for and pray for you. Love, always.

To my Brothers, you are the ultimate a sister could ever ask for and more. I tell people all the time how I won the sibling lottery. I wish I could open my heart so you could understand how much I love and respect you. Life would not mean anything without you. Thank you for being the best uncles in the world. Thank you for your trials and triumphs. I pray for your peace, prosperity and joy. I love you forever. God Bless you.

Mommy, I love you with all of me. Thank you for supporting me even when you quite didn't understand what I was doing or why. Thank you to you and Gabey for stepping in for us in the moments I was too proud or ashamed to ask for help, in the moments I couldn't go one more step alone. Thank you for insisting you take the girls for a day or two to give me the time I needed to take care of business. I value that to no end. Thank you for your love. Thank you for giving me the best day of my life (Knott's and the Meghan punch) and the best summer ever, 2023, in San Clemente when we really got acquainted with the community. Gabey, thank you for my beautiful bicycle. Momma, thank you for always listening and grounding me. I see that is how you show me your love. Thank you for introducing me to the crack (it's an appetizer, folks), for allowing me to drown your culinary masterpieces in A1 sauce and for being my escape. That freedom has opened me up creatively in so many ways. I finally feel seen, safe and at peace and I'll never settle for less. I love y'all!!!

To my sweet girls who have shared me with my art so selflessly, patiently and graciously, Mama loves you more than anything in the world!!! You are divine art in your own right and every late night, every insanely early morning, every sacrifice, every push was all worth it. You are my fuel to make things happen. You are my reasons "why". Thank you for your love. Thank you for being you! Thank you for taking this journey with me. You are the best life companions a mama could ever ask for. No other beings on this earth but you four really know what it took to create this book. I love you with every part of my being. You are my life, my heart, my all. Anything & everything for y'all! Girls World! Uncle Harry! LOL XOXO God Bless you, my loves.

KAYLEE "LADY K DAY" HANNAH
was born in Texas, raised in Southern California and,
with roots in and a deep love for Los Angeles, calls the
city of Chino her home.

As a musical poet, she plays various instruments, sings
and raps. She has performed on the stages of House
of Blues Anaheim, Art Share L.A., World Stage
Performance Gallery, Sims Library of Poetry,
Planet Health Compton and at SWAAM at
The Barbara Morrison Performing Arts
Center.

On a mission to rattle cages and
burst out of the boxes society
clings to for safety and comfort,
she is a believer in raw honesty,
open vulnerability and life altering
love. Her aim is to spark a "kinder
than necessary" movement with
her art and leave a lasting legacy
for her daughters — who are her
entire world and best friends.